THE LIFE
OF
MAXIM GORKY

MAXIM GORKY
(ALEXEI MAXIMOVICH PESHKOV)
1936

A. ROSKIN

THE LIFE OF MAXIM GORKY

*Translated from the Russian
by
D. L. Fromberg*

Fredonia Books
Amsterdam, The Netherlands

The Life of Maxim Gorky

by
A. Roskin

ISBN: 1-4101-0148-7

Copyright © 2003 by Fredonia Books

Reprinted from the 1944 edition

Fredonia Books
Amsterdam, The Netherlands
http://www.fredoniabooks.com

All rights reserved, including the right to reproduce this book, or portions thereof, in any form.

CONTENTS

			Page
Chapter	I:	CHILDHOOD	5
Chapter	II:	IN KAZAN	19
		1. "Wrangler"	19
		2. Two Bakeries	22
		3. "An Incident in the Life of Makar"	27
		4. The Village Shop	29
Chapter	III:	THE RAILWAY NIGHT WATCHMAN	31
Chapter	IV:	"THE SONG OF THE OLD OAK"	35
Chapter	V:	WANDERINGS	41
Chapter	VI:	THE FIRST STORY	46
Chapter	VII:	YEGUDIL KHLAMIDA	49
Chapter	VIII:	FAME	54
Chapter	IX:	METEKH CASTLE AND THE NIZHNI-NOVGOROD GAOL	58
Chapter	X:	NIGHTINGALES AND SPIES	66
Chapter	XI:	ON THE STAGE OF THE ART THEATRE	71
Chapter	XII:	THREE REVOLUTIONS	77
Chapter	XIII:	WRITER AND FIGHTER	89

Chapter I

CHILDHOOD

> "Sorrow we breathe, with sorrow we are encompassed."
>
> (*A proverb*)

A rainy day, a deserted corner of a churchyard, slimy earth, a coffin, two frogs on the coffin lid—this was all that was associated in Gorky's mind with his father.

And had it not been for his grandmother, Gorky would probably never have known anything about him. A plain Russian man, he had vanished from this life without a trace, leaving no papers or letters behind him, not even a picture of himself.

From all that his grandmother had told him about his father Alosha in the end had drawn one conclusion, namely, that children were made to be thrashed: Alosha's life was being made a misery by Vassili Kashirin—his grandfather on his mother's side; his father's life had been made a misery by Savvati Peshkov—his grandfather on his father's side.

This Savvati Peshkov, a soldier, had been a terrible man.

He had served for many years in the army, rising to officer's rank, but for the brutal way in which he had treated his subordinates he had been deprived of his commission and exiled to Siberia.

It was more than probable that Savvati Peshkov had been guilty of truly appalling outrages but, after all, he had served in the army at a time when a brutal attitude towards the lower ranks was rated as an undoubted virtue on the part of an officer.

Deprived of the power he had wielded over his subordinates, Savvati Peshkov had vented all that was most malevolent in his nature on his son Maxim—Gorky's father.

Time and again Maxim had attempted to run away from home. The old soldier had set after him with dogs and every time he ran him down he had thrashed him to within an inch of his life.

When Savvati Peshkov died Maxim—Gorky's father—had left his native parts and after tramping through the whole of Siberia had at last come to the Volga, to the city of Nizhni-Novgorod. Here he had entered a cabinet maker's shop as an apprentice and learned the trades of cabinet making, upholstering and paperhanging.

The shop adjoined a dyeing establishment owned by a man named Kashirin, whose daughter, Varya, subsequently became Maxim Peshkov's wife.

After his marriage Maxim Savvatievich had gone to live with the Kashirins. It was in their home, a typical lower middle class cottage, on one of the dullest and dreariest streets in Nizhni-Novgorod, that a son had been born to the Peshkovs in 1868 whom they had named Alexei, or Alosha as he was known to everybody.

In *My Childhood* Gorky devotes but a few pages to his father. Yet, reading these pages, one instinctively realizes what a splendid man Maxim Savvatievich must have been and why Gorky chose his father's name for his pen name. Maxim Savvatievich—the future author's father—was hounded in his youth like a hare, and persecuted as though he was a soldier in a penal company. And yet for all that he had faced the world with a kindly and good-humoured smile.

The Kashirins, however, resembled Savvati Peshkov in their sheer brutality. They hated one another with an undying, bitter hatred.

"There's another row at the Kashirin's!" the street urchins would shout, and this cry would be heard almost every day.

When they quarrelled they usually raised such a racket that the whole street soon became aware of it. But when they were dead set against anyone they acted noiselessly, furtively. That was how Gorky's uncles, the sons of Vassili Vassilievich Kashirin, his grandfather and the owner of the dyeing establishment, beat their wives— so that nobody was any the wiser.

Maxim Savvatievich had felt a stranger in this house and that was why everybody had hated him so. One winter's day the Kashirin brothers had thrown him into a hole in the ice. Maxim Savvatievich had barely managed to save himself.

He had not breathed a word about this to anybody; he had merely left the Kashirin's house.

The Peshkovs had travelled down the Volga to Astrakhan, where Maxim Savvatievich had been offered employment.

It was while they were living there that misfortune had overtaken the Peshkov family. When Alosha was four years old he had fallen ill with the cholera, which was a frequent visitor to this semi-Asiatic town. The boy recovered, but his father, Maxim Savvatievich, who had contracted the disease from him, died.

So Alosha found himself back again in Nizhni-Novgorod, in the Kashirin household, amongst the people who had tried to murder his father.

Alosha well remembered the long trip up river, the lengthy journey by boat past the woods, touched by the hand of autumn, past the steep yellow banks and the miniature towns which looked like toys in the distance....

The Kashirins had moved to a new district, to a squat, dirty-reddish house with a hanging roof and bulging windows.

Life in the Kashirin household was a never-ending round of reproaches, senseless abuse, ruthless floggings, money-grabbing and dreary supplications to God.

More than anyone else Alosha disliked his grandfather, Vassili Vassilievich, with his reddish beard, green eyes, and hands that seemed to be smeared with blood, the dye had so eaten into the skin. His abuse and prayers, his jests and moralizing all merged in some strange way into a rasping, caustic whine that ate like rust into one's heart.

Alosha felt instinctively that his grandfather was his main enemy and he was not mistaken: he was cruelly treated by all the Kashirins alike, but the man who made him suffer more than anyone else was Vassili Vassilievich.

It was a frightful life, but more frightful than anything else was the fact that all around everything seemed to be as dark as in the Kashirin household.

Alosha would look through the window into the street. To the right loomed the big, yellow barracks of the convict gangs. To the left was Prison Square and the grey building of the gaol with the four towers, one at each corner.

Between the barracks and the gaol, amidst a sea of mud, stood rows of houses—dun-coloured, green, white. And in every one of them, just as in the Kashirin household, people fought and squabbled because the pudding was burnt or the milk had curdled, in every one of them the same petty interests prevailed—about pots and pans and samovars and pancakes—and in every one of them people just as religiously celebrated birthdays and commemoration days, guzzling until they were ready to burst and swilling like hogs.

It was of Nizhni-Novgorod that people said: "Houses of stone, men of iron."

And these men of iron believed that the life they were living was the one true life, deep-rooted and firmly established on earth for all time.

Alosha Peshkov felt as though he were at the bottom of a deep pit. He was still young when he first came to hate the smug philistines with their cares and worries over a copper and their talk and interests which were alike as two coppers.

He tried to fence himself off from these people, to have a corner somewhere to himself which would be his very own.

In the Kashirin's dismal backyard, as far away as possible from the vats of dye and the rags on the clotheslines, Alosha cultivated a small plot and planted it with flowers which grew quite well. But one day, when he went to water them, he saw that his flower-bed had been uprooted, the flowers trampled underfoot and the Kashirin's hog, which had kicked down the gate with its hind legs, wallowing in the middle of them.

In just the same way did people break into Gorky's childhood. With the same callous indifference they trampled underfoot everything that the lad held dear.

But there were also happy moments in his childhood.

His greatest joy was his grandmother—Akulina Ivanovna—who years later became so dear and close to millions of readers of *My Childhood*.

It was Akulina Ivanovna who fostered Alosha Peshkov's simple, but wonderful belief in human happiness and who prevented the Kashirin gloom from overwhelming the lad's soul.

Her wordly wisdom was not the grudging, time-blackened wisdom born of long suffering.

Everything about granny was expressive of her own unique nature, fine and warmhearted; and this warmth manifested itself in every word and every movement, in the way, for instance, she took a pinch of snuff from her black, silver-engraved snuffbox or how, with an aged but steady hand, she picked some familiar herb while out for a stroll.

Grandmother was sorry for people, had a knowledge of woodcraft and loved to weave tales. And this sympathy, knowledge and love she passed on to her grandson in words that were like a garland of flowers.

She told Alosha about the Kashirins and the past, about the medicinal qualities of herbs and the terrible stories about Old Mother Usta or the brigand mother's grief. His grandmother's stories were his first, unwritten book—a book which Gorky loved and treasured all his life.

He heard stories from nurse Yevgenya too. Nurse was fond of daring stories about God and priests. God lived on earth and went from village to village, clumsily interposing in people's affairs in a way which only showed him to be obtuse and sometimes malignant.

And the people in nurse's stories were also bad—judges who bartered justice as though it was a yard of cloth or a pound of meat, landowners who amazed him with their cruelty, a cruelty which seemed to have no rhyme or reason, merchants who were so miserly that one of them even sold his wife and children to the Tatars for the extra fifty kopecks which he needed to make up a round thousand....

Alosha was ready to believe in nurse's stories, the more so since the mercenary judges, cruel landowners and grasping merchants were all so familiar to him, resembling in every way the Kashirins and the people who lived in the neighbouring houses.

But his grandmother's and the nurse's stories also convinced him that there were good people somewhere on earth.

One day just such a man actually did appear near at hand—in the Kashirin's house itself. A lodger moved into the small room next to the kitchen and turned it into a laboratory in which he conducted various experiments. The queer thing about this round-shouldered, gaunt-looking, bespectacled man was not that he was forever busy with copper scales, spirit stove and charts, but that he never took any money for his trouble and did not show the least interest in money.

He was a quiet man and very lonely. The Kashirins, naturally, could not stand the sight of him, and in the end grandfather Kashirin gave him notice to leave.

The lodger disappeared together with his scales and other accessories, but Alosha never forgot him.

He was firmly convinced now that the good people in the stories were not just a fairy tale. They had to be sought everywhere wherever people differed from those who lived in Polevaya Street or Kanatnaya Street—the streets in Nizhni-Novgorod where Gorky spent his childhood.

But to search meant casting adrift from home, getting as far away as possible, disappearing just as the lodger had disappeared. And Alosha was ready to go with anybody, only to be going somewhere, not to live in an atmosphere of stagnancy....

Often people in the drab uniforms of convicts passed by the Kashirin's house. They would march under escort to the wharf and embark on a steamer which took them far away. Alosha envied them. Better to be going somewhere even under convoy, with chains on one's ankles, but still to be going somewhere....

One day a batch of convicts passed down the street. Alosha was struck by the forbidding appearance of one of the men, who had a large red scar on his forehead and an ear that was frightfully mutilated.

Alosha followed him on the sidewalk. Suddenly the convict shouted to him merrily:

"Come on lad, come for a ride with us!"

Alosha immediately ran up to the convict, and if the

warder had not chased him away, he would have gone with the man—it made no difference where, only to be going somewhere, never to return.

He went home and life jogged on in the same humdrum fashion. Only the houses changed in which the Kashirins lived. From the dirty-reddish house in Uspensky Street his grandfather moved to Polevaya, into a large house with a wine cellar in the basement, and from there to Kanatnaya Street, into a house with claret red walls and blue shutters.

Alosha was bored and gloomy. At times he tried to overcome this feeling by giving way to fits of unrestrained mischievousness. He would climb on to the roof and stuff up the chimneys or pour salt into the soup or blow dust through a paper funnel into the works of the kitchen clock.

Why did he do it? He himself did not know.

But at times the brutality which he witnessed on every hand roused another feeling in him—hatred. Once when Alosha saw his stepfather beat his mother and kick her in the chest, he snatched up a knife and stabbed him in the ribs.

Gorky was ten years of age when he went out into the world to earn his own living. His mother had died; his stepfather had gambled away everything at cards and lost his job, his grandfather was bankrupt.

He had to start working for a living.

He was in turn an errand-boy in a shoestore, a dishwasher on a steamboat, a draftsman's apprentice, an iconpainter's apprentice, a rag-and-bone man and a birdcatcher.

In the shoestore the proprietor made Gorky's life a misery with his unsavoury stories about his women clients, and the shop assistant with his bullying, while Sasha—one of the Kashirin boys who was also employed there—would stick needles in the shoes so that Gorky, whose job it was to dust them, would be always pricking his fingers.

Gorky stood behind the counter and looked out of the window. It was a frosty day and only a few people were abroad. Horses trudged slowly through the snowdrifts, from a nearby belfry came the monotonous pealing of church bells, and all he wished for just then was that his employer, with his bleary, dim-sighted eyes, would pick on him for some trivial offence and give him the sack.

He waited in vain. But one day while Gorky was warming up some soup, he upset the pot and scalded his hands so badly that he had to be sent to hospital. After leaving the hospital he did not go back to the shoestore but apprenticed himself to a draftsman, a distant relative of his.

Here it was even worse than in the shoestore. His new employer did not teach him a thing about the trade. Gorky chopped and carried wood, washed pots and pans, scrubbed floors, cleaned the samovar and the copper kitchen utensils, went to the market and ran on errands to the grocery store.

But it was not this that was so bad, for Gorky did everything he was told willingly enough. The trouble was that the womenfolk, the draftsman's wife and mother-in-law, worried the life out of him, abused him and thrashed him, taking advantage of their dual right of being both his employers and relatives.

In the shoestore Gorky had patiently waited to be sacked. He left the draftsman of his own accord—scuttled away like a mouse in a cellar.

For several days he roamed the streets of Nizhni-Novgorod, hung about the wharves and the longshoremen until at last he managed to get a job as a dishwasher on the steamboat *Dobri*.

The *Dobri* was a prison ship—she used to tow the barges transporting convicts.

Gorky had hardly more liberty than the convicts themselves. From six in the morning until midnight he was kept busy washing pots and pans and plates and cleaning knives and forks.

But for all that he much preferred his new job to Porkhunov's shoestore, or Sergeyev's drafting office. In front of him stretched the broad tranquil river. From the deck he could see dark forests and empty meadows, strange towns far and few between and solitary villages lost in the vast plains. Nature here was close at hand, almost within his reach, and she reminded him of liberty and of that splendid summer he and his grandmother had once spent when they had gone off into the woods together and she had taught him how to pick mushrooms and medicinal herbs and to search for squirrel's caches stocked with nuts.

Gorky had come to love the woods during these outings, and it was this that induced him later on to give up his job as a dishwasher on the steamboat and become a birdcatcher.

He bought a net, a hoop and traps and made a number of cages. In the forest ravines he stalked red-headed goldfinches, strange little martins, screeching crossbills and vicious but shrewd titmice.

The birds he trapped were sold by his grandmother at the market. In this way the two of them, Gorky and his grandmother, lived for a time on what they found in and about the woods.

The summer came to an end, the birds flew away and they had to go back to town. Working for various employers he once again lost his liberty and would often be parted from his grandmother for a long time.

But he found something else to uphold him.

This was books.

Gorky's road to the world of books was tortuous and difficult. His grandfather had taught him to read from old church books and then his mother had given him lessons from "secular works." But this schooling, drilled into him by means of threats, abuse and canings, had been no less harsh than his "schooling" at the shoestore or draftsman's office.

And in the school which Gorky had attended for a while, the boys had teased him as a ragpicker and tramp, while the teacher, a ruddy, sour-faced man, had for some reason or other taken a special delight in picking on him.

But when Gorky at long last did discover the world of books, they entered his life as something big, vital and joyous.

One of the first books he acquired was Hans Andersen's *Fairy Tales*.

He began to read *The Nightingale*. The story appealed to him from the very first line:

"In China all the inhabitants are Chinese, and the Emperor is also Chinese."

But Andersen's *Fairy Tales* were merely a stroke of good luck. He did not pick and choose his books but read everything that fell into his hands, everything that he got for nothing from chance friends or for money at second-hand book-shops.

The books that Gorky read in his childhood were as motley as the people he met on his path.

The first man who supplied Gorky with books was the cook of the *Dobri*—an ex-non-commissioned officer of a Guards regiment by the name of Smuri.

From a cabin trunk clamped with iron hoops the old soldier brought to light books which bore the most intriguing titles: *Omirov's Precepts, The Memoirs of a Gunner, Lord Sedengally's Letters*.... At all events the ship's cook was Gorky's first teacher, inasmuch as it was he who inculcated in him a love for books.

Gorky procured books wherever he could—from secondary schoolboys and choirboys, shopkeepers and iconpainters—voraciously devouring cheap thrillers and adventure stories translated into the Russian. Amongst all this trash Gorky happened to chance on books by the great French writers—Balzac and Flaubert.

One Sunday, ensconced on the roof of a shed where nobody could disturb him, he read Flaubert's *Un Coeur simple*, the story of how a cook lived her artless life.

The simple words, knitted together into simple phrases, moved him, stirred him and the story seemed to him to be little short of a miracle.

Time and again he caught himself holding up some strange book to the light as though trying to find between the lines the reason for such a miracle, but without success. But now other books began to replace the favourite literature of the cooks and shopkeepers and choirboys, books which he learned to love with a deep and tender love: Pushkin and Gogol, Turgenev and Lermontov.

He very early developed a fine and sensitive feeling for genuine literature.

In one humorous magazine published in St. Petersburg Gorky chanced on a short story which particularly appealed to him. He felt an impulse to try and write just as well.

Under the story was the strange pen name: Antosha Chekhonte.

Gorky asked a secondary schoolboy with whom he was chummy who this Chekhonte was, but the lad remarked importantly that it would be far better for him to read serious books and not waste his time on comic magazines.

This was the first story which Gorky read by the as yet unknown Chekhov, who subsequently became his favourite author and close friend.

To Gorky life seemed a prison cell and books—the birds whose singing reached the men behind the bars.

In one periodical he chanced upon a portrait of the famous scientist Faraday and reading the accompanying article ascertained that the latter had begun life as an ordinary worker.

Gorky was astounded. It seemed incredible to him.

MAXIM GORKY
St. Petersburg—1907

He made a point of finding out whether there were any other notable people who had begun life as workers.

Gorky did not find any more data on the subject in the periodical magazines but somebody mentioned to him that Stephenson—the inventor of the locomotive engine—had also been a worker.

Gorky did not strive towards fame. All he dreamed of was a life that would be fit for a human being. At one time he thought that he would find the glamour of real life on the stage.

His first visit to the theatre was a matter of chance. It happened at a fair. Shchedrin's *The Golovlyov Family* was being staged in a red brick building. The well-known actor Andreyev-Burlak played the part of Judas Golovlyov. Gorky was ready to shed tears of hatred. He felt like rushing on to the stage and choking the life out of Judas. Only then did he realize what a mighty influence the theatre had.

After the play Gorky wandered all night through the meadows behind the fair. A drunkard accosted him and hit him on the head but he hardly took any notice of the man, so engrossed was he with what he had seen.

He felt a desire to go on the stage. His wish was almost fulfilled. He found a job in a theatre, not as an actor, true, but as a super.

The first play in which Gorky took part was a drama of a sort with singing and dancing, entitled "Christopher Columbus or The Discovery of America." Gorky played the part of a Red Indian. All he had to do was poke Spaniards in the stomach with a wooden spear, but when he himself was "run through" by a sword he completely forgot that he had to reel back and fall.

Gorky did not become an actor. However much the theatre may at times grip the attention of the playgoer, life behind the scenes of a provincial theatre was dull and crude. The hero, who had only a moment ago knelt at the feet of his beloved, shouted at her:

"Why the devil must you keep on sticking pins all over yourself?"

And the benevolent father, who had been shedding tears on the stage at the unhappy lot of his daughter, hissed at her behind the scenes:

"You dolt, you forgot your lines again!"

At the rehearsals the stage director would treat the supers like galley slaves. He called Gorky a cussed nincompoop and an unscrupulous lout. The dark auditorium seemed like a vast, deep vault. And, once again, his dreams shattered, Gorky abandoned the stage.

He made up his mind to study.

The secondary schoolboy who had told him about Stephenson advised him to go to Kazan, where there was a university.

And so Gorky left his native parts and went to Kazan. It was without any feelings of regret that he left Nizhni-Novgorod with its dingy attics and basements and people.

Gorky at the time was fifteen years of age.

Chapter II

IN KAZAN

1. "*Wrangler*"

"If anybody had proposed to me:

"'Go and study, but on condition that you'll be publicly birched every Sunday on Nikolayevsky Square,' I would most likely have agreed."

So Gorky wrote in his reminiscences.

Nothing, however, came of his longing to study.

When Gorky arrived in Kazan he realized that he, a down-at-heels tramp from Nizhni-Novgorod without a roof over his head, would never be able to enter the university.

Something else, however, was in store for him—the cellars on the outskirts of the city, the riverside wharves, underground political circles, hobnobbing with *bosyaks* (tramps), policemen, students and revolutionaries. This was the university which Gorky entered, and the schooling that he received in this university was such as could never be forgotten. . . .

Gorky found lodgings of a sort in the basement of a broken-down house on a bleak strip of wasteland and a job at the riverside wharves at Ustya. He was paid twenty kopecks a day.

His new companions were a motley crowd, the usual denizens of the wharves—longshoremen, pickpockets, beggars and the still more nondescript inhabitants of the "Crystal Palace." This was the name that was for some reason or other given to the dilapidated old building, presumably because there was not a single whole pane in the windows.

The "Crystal Palace" was the rendezvous of the Kazan tramps. Here an ex-student who had been expelled from the university rubbed shoulders with an old ragpicker who had served a term of ten years, with a beggar who earlier in his career had been a veterinary surgeon and a vagrant who had once been butler to a provincial governor. Their pasts were utterly different, but their present lot was the same—a hungry and intolerable existence.

Gorky found them strange enough and often quite unaccountable, but for all that he preferred these outcasts to the people who lived in their smug little houses with their iron-bound chests and tiny double windows trimmed with coloured paper. The *bosyaks* drank and fought and stole, but none of them were mean or miserly or whined at their lot, and all of them jeered contemptuously at their "betters."

One of them once stole a pair of first-rate hunting boots. They decided to sell them and buy drinks all round with the proceeds. But another *bosyak*, a sick man who had been beaten up a few days before by the police, proposed that they should only sell the uppers for drinks and give the rest of the boots to the "student chap," who was going around almost barefoot.

"He'll catch cold," he said, "and peg out and, after all, he's not a bad guy."

Many of them reminded Gorky of the picturesque individuals he had read of in adventure books.

But it was not only adventure book heroes that gripped Gorky's imagination. He dreamed of something more significant. And it was this that constantly drove him to new people, new ideas and strange books.

Some of Gorky's friends once took him to a small grocery shop on the outskirts of the city. The proprietor of the shop, Andrei Derenkov, was a revolutionary. He did a moderate trade in sugar and candles, sweetmeats and soap, but in a back room, on one of the walls of which hung a portrait of Hertzen, he had hidden away a store of forbidden books.

From then on works by scientists, thinkers and revolutionaries began to replace the novels and adventure stories which Gorky had been insatiably devouring.

Through Derenkov's shop Gorky got in touch with the secret students' associations. The members of these associations studied works on history and political economy, read papers and noisily debated the fate of the revolution in Russia.

This was a free university of the revolutionary youth and Gorky learned more in it than he could ever have acquired at the Imperial Kazan University.

It was in this university that Gorky became acquainted with the theories of Adam Smith, the writings of Chernyshevsky and the works of Karl Marx. Marx's *Capital* was a bibliographical rarity in those days and what went the rounds was a handwritten copy of the first chapter. . . .

Once, when the Kazan police searched Gorky's lodgings, they found amongst his belongings an exercise book full of jottings. It was fortunate for him that this exercise book contained excerpts not from Marx but from a book of a more innocent nature—Mirtov-Lavrov's *Modern Teachings on Ethics and Their History*.

The police, however, did not fail to report this at once to the authorities in Gorky's home town, Nizhni-Novgorod. The fact that this working man who chopped wood and did odd jobs at the wharves for a living read scientific works and made excerpts from them seemed highly suspicious.

In the underground associations Gorky was nicknamed "Wrangler" not only for his deep bass voice and broad accent. He read papers and took part in the lengthy debates that lasted until the small hours. The opinions he expressed were not mere book learning but his own mature thoughts. He had a deeper knowledge of life than many of his comrades and he would often astonish his listeners with the unexpectedness and trenchant force of his comments.

"You're off the track, brother!" Gorky once angrily reproached one of his mentors.

Many of the things that Gorky gleaned from his reading were only too familiar to him. The authors of the treatises on political economy described the wretched lot of the workers, a lot that Gorky knew only too well from his own experience.

In Kazan he had to go through the most difficult of all the universities which life held in store for him.

2. Two Bakeries

"The story savours strongly of dough, has a flavour of cracknels about it."
(*From one of Chekhov's letters to Gorky*)

Autumn came. The last steamers of the season hastened to their winter berths. The wharves became deserted, there was no more work to be had on the river.

Gorky wandered about the silent Ustya district, past empty booths and boarded up buildings.

He went hungry, slept where he could, even under an overturned boat on the river bank, and became gloomily convinced that autumn was the worst time for a homeless waif.

Gorky was ready to turn his hand to anything if only it would put a roof over his head.

He started to work for three rubles a month as a baker's helper in Semyonov's pretzel establishment.

Semyonov's bakery was located in a basement. The windows of the pretzel establishment looked out on an areaway. The owner had them set with iron bars so that the workers could not give any bread away to beggars.

Here, in this basement, Gorky had to work for fourteen hours a day fashioning pretzels in the form of a letter "B." He had long since become inured to hard physical labour but, strong and wiry as he was for his age, the back-breaking work in Semyonov's establishment taxed his strength.

At times Gorky felt as though all the three storeys of the building in which the pretzel establishment had its premises were resting on his shoulders.

The people who lived in the house called Semyonov's workers "gaolbirds."

Semyonov not only sweated his "lads" for fourteen hours a day, but never missed a chance of bullying them, beating them, fining them and punishing them as if his bakery were really a prison.

Gorky was not surprised so much by the brutal way in which Semyonov treated his workers—young as he was he had seen more than enough of that already. What astonished him was something else—the meekness with which they took it all and their readiness even to go into raptures over Semyonov's wiles. Gorky held different opinions on bosses and he boldly expressed them to his fellow-workers.

Once Semyonov overheard him talking to the men.

"What are you gabbing about, 'Wrangler'?" he demanded.

Gorky was punished: for a whole week he was put to kneading dough.

But "Wrangler" knew how to stand up for his rights as a human being. Semyonov had to face the fact that down below, in his basement, he had a man whose spirit he would never succeed in breaking.

But even his work could not tear Gorky away from his books. He knocked together a makeshift book stand out of odd bits of firewood. In this way he could read and lay out the pretzels on the racks at the same time.

One day Semyonov suddenly came into the bakery and caught Gorky reading a book by Tolstoy. He wanted to throw it into the fire.

"Don't you dare burn that book!" Gorky exclaimed, catching Semyonov by the arm.

He said it in such a meaning tone that Semyonov returned the book without a word and left the basement.

On another occasion, when Semyonov was bullying the men in a particularly exasperating manner, Gorky calmly took him by the ear and tweaked it. Semyonov was so accustomed to the workers taking everything lying down that he was more astounded than incensed.

Gorky not only stood up for his own rights; he also tried to defend those of his comrades. In the wooden chest which he kept on top of the oven he had several well-thumbed books of verse. Sometimes he would read to Semyonov's "gaolbirds" the lines of the poet:

> *How lofty, oh man,*
> *is your destiny. . . .*

Gorky wanted to make the workers remind their boss of this lofty destiny of theirs. He tried to organize a strike but nothing came of it.

His friendship with the revolutionaries enabled him to give up his job at Semyonov's establishment.

Andrei Derenkov opened a bakery, the profits of which were to be devoted to revolutionary work. The establishment needed a baker's assistant and Gorky was the very man they required for the job.

He moved his few belongings from Semyonov's to Derenkov's He kneaded dough, set the loaves in the oven and delivered freshly baked rolls to the students' dining room. And often in his bread basket Gorky would have hidden away revolutionary literature which he would furtively pass on to one of the students together with his rolls. . . .

Derenkov's bakery adjoined the gendarmerie. The gendarmes, in their blue uniforms, would climb the fence and drop in to the bakery for rolls.

Derenkov's establishment was under suspicion.

"Are you fond of reading?" a gendarme by the name of Nikiforich asked Gorky. "What books, for example, do you like best?"

Nikiforich would invite the baker's helper to his sentry-box and turn the conversation to students and enemies of the people.

"An invisible thread," Nikiforich explained, "emanates like a fine gossamer web from the heart of His Imperial Majesty Alexander III, Tsar of all the Russias, etc., etc. And this thread passes through their most gracious Excellencies, the Ministers of the Crown, through their Excellencies the Governor-Generals of the various Gubernias and through all the other officers and servants in His Majesty's service down to the last rank-and-file soldier. It is this thread that links all and sundry and enmeshes all and sundry. It is the invisible strength of this thread that binds together for ever and ever His Majesty's realm. Understand?"

Gorky understood. He was beginning to feel this invisible thread more and more—the thread of espionage and informing.

The entire country was enmeshed in this web. Through its agency the government plucked revolutionaries from underground and threw them into prison or sent them to convict labour camps.

This invisible thread entangled people who were weaker, people who saw the injustice of the existing order but lacked the courage to pit themselves against it. A void formed around every person who would not bend and it was not easy to escape this void.

Gorky, too, gradually began to feel the void close round him.

Conditions at Derenkov's bakery were better than at Semyonov's pretzel establishment but here, too, Gorky was busy all day long, sometimes till late at night. Dead tired after the day's work he would come home to his tiny den and there, drawing the small oil lamp with its dull blue glass closer to his book, settled down to read.

During these nocturnal hours Gorky accumulated a vast store of knowledge. An overturned box served him as a table and on it, next to a volume of Pushkin, lay the physiologist Sechenov's work *Reflexes of the Brain*.

And often, closing a book, he would dream of a different life, cultured and full of interest, which he believed must exist somewhere.

He longed to confide these thoughts of his to someone.

With mingled feelings of alarm and hope and regardless of the danger Nikiforich had hinted at, Gorky turned to those whose lives were bound up with the revolution.

He met with sympathy in the underground circles. But the attitude towards him there was somewhat condescending, as intellectuals often are to self-taught men.

And that was how they usually introduced Gorky:

"A self-taught man . . . from the people."

They marvelled at him but more often than not listened indifferently to what he had to say and sometimes even poked fun at him.

Sometimes Gorky would make an attempt to broach the subjects of his thoughts.

"Oh, chuck it!" they would cut him short.

And Gorky would drop the subject.

He began to keep a notebook in which he jotted down poems of his own composition in between passages copied from books he had read. He wrote about his unfortunate friend—the glass-blower Anatole, about the thawing snow which trickled down in a turbid stream into the basement of the bakery, but above all about the Volga he loved.

Gorky never showed this notebook to anybody.

3. *"An Incident in the Life of Makar"*

> "You, madam, undoubtedly know some remedy for a toothache, don't you? But I have a toothache in my heart. That's a bad ache, but an ounce of lead and some of that tooth powder invented by Berthold Schwartz is an excellent remedy for it."
>
> *(Heinrich Heine)*

A letter came from Nizhni-Novgorod telling Gorky that his grandmother had died, the only near and dear friend he had had in the world. . . .

Autumn came with its incessant rain. It seemed as though the invisible web Nikiforich had spoken of in his sentry-box had entangled the whole of ailing nature.

Gorky recalled the past, his grandmother, their wonderful outings to the woods, his books—the good and bright sides of his life, while all the rest was as depressing as this interminable autumn.

At night melancholy strains filtered from Gorky's tiny den. Heavy at heart he took to playing the violin....

This was a year during which very many people committed suicide. One student wrote in a farewell letter about a "quicker exit from life".

Some of Gorky's friends also sought a "quicker exit from life." Muzykantsky, a shock-headed, sad-faced student shot himself. . . .

On December 14, 1887, the Kazan newspaper *The Volzhski Vestnik* carried the following item:

"On December 12, at 8 p. m., in Podlyuzhnaya Street, on the bank of the River Kazanka, Alexei Maximov Peshkov, an artisan from the city of Nizhni-Novgorod, shot himself with a revolver in the left side with the object of taking his own life. Peshkov was immediately taken to the Zemstvo hospital, where the doctor who attended him stated that the wound was dangerous. In a note found on him Peshkov wrote that he held no one to blame for his death."

The reason why "Alexei Maximov Peshkov, an artisan from the city of Nizhni-Novgorod, shot himself with a revolver in the left side," was explained by Gorky himself a quarter of a century later in his story: *An Incident in the Life of Makar*. This was merely an incident, but it was a tragic incident, and it served as an additional instance of the incredible difficulties that beset Gorky's path in life.

Resolved to take his own life Gorky went to the market and bought a heavy Tula revolver for three rubles.

That same night Gorky made his way to the outskirts of the town. . . .

He was found lying in the snow, on the edge of the river bank, and taken to the hospital.

A queer note was found in his pocket:

"I lay the blame of my death on the German poet Heine, who invented a toothache of the heart. I am attaching herewith my passport which I obtained specifically for this occasion. Please make a post-mortem examination of my remains and ascertain what devil has possessed me of late.

"It will be seen from my passport that I am A. Peshkov, but from this note, I hope, nothing will be seen."

The doctor's verdict was that the wounded man would die within three days. These words penetrated Gorky's half-conscious mind.

"No, I won't die," he said.

The professor lost his temper. He was apparently of the opinion that the sick man was conducting himself in a way that was hardly polite.

Gorky did not die.

During his slow and difficult recovery he was visited in hospital by his old comrades, the workers from Semyonov's pretzel establishment. From them he heard words of comfort, words that were simple, tender and human. And Gorky felt that "the toothache in his heart" had passed and that he wanted to go on living.

4. The Village Shop

He went back to Derenkov's bakery, but not for long.

From time to time a man by the name of Mikhail Antonovich Romas would drop in to the bakery. The son of a locksmith and himself a former railway worker, this old revolutionary who had already served a sentence of ten years exile gave the impression of being a man of uncommon strength and calm determination.

Romas became interested in Gorky. He realized that the baker's helper needed guidance and support and invited him to Krasnovydovo, a village on the Volga, where he kept a small shop. This shop served Romas as a retreat in the country where he carried on revolutionary propaganda amongst the peasantry.

And so Gorky went to stay with Romas.

At Krasnovydovo he had an opportunity of closely observing peasant life for the first time. And every passing day he spent there left him more and more heavy at heart.

In many of the books which Gorky had read the muzhiks had been portrayed as dreamy and simple-hearted folks. At Krasnovydovo he saw something entirely different—blind hatred and wolfish greed. Three families went for each other with clubs with the result that an old woman's arm was broken and a youngster's head split open—and all for the sake of a cracked earthern pot. And hardly a week passed but something of the same nature took place.

The well-to-do villagers of Krasnovydovo hated Romas and his shop. Of an evening a crowd would gather near the shop and the comments made about him were far from complimentary.

Shortly after Gorky's arrival, the kulaks began to grow active.

Izot, a peasant who had been on friendly terms with Romas, was found dead with a broken skull on the banks of the Volga.

Then somebody fired at Romas with a shotgun.

After that the kulaks blew up the stove in Romas' house by filling one of his logs with a charge of gun powder. Finally they set fire to the shop and the house. Gorky was trapped by the flames in the attic. He wrapped a sheepskin coat round him and jumped out of the window.

Romas' shop was burned down to the ground. Gorky had to look for another roof over his head.

He left Krasnovydovo. Together with his friend Barinov, Gorky made his way down river to Astrakhan. They were a long time getting the e, now stowing away on passenger steamboats, now working their passage as bargehands. At last they reached the Caspian. It was here that Gorky had his first glimpse of the sea. Here, too, the recent baker and shopkeeper's assistant began to work as a fisherman.

Chapter III

THE RAILWAY NIGHT WATCHMAN

Kazan seemed chilly and uninviting to Gorky on his return from the Caspian. Derenkov's shop had closed down. Many of his old friends had also vanished from the horizon.

Unable to find a place in town, Gorky took on a job as night watchman at Dobrinka, a dull little railway station.

One of the dreams he had cherished ever since he had been a child was to get away from town, to live in some forester's hut or out-of-the-way by-station.

And now this forlorn childish wish came true. But even here he found no peace of mind.

Every night, from six in the evening till six in the morning, Gorky, stick in hand, would make the rounds of the freight sheds, keeping watch over the sacks of flour. Gorky saw to it that the flour was not stolen by the Cossacks of the near-by *stanitsas*.* But the Cossacks were not the only ones who tried to help themselves. The stationmaster himself was not averse to taking his share. He was a big husky man with bulging eyes and a black beard. Everybody called him "Afrikan". Whenever freight cars stopped at Dobrinka en route from the South, from the Caspian, Afrikan would break into them, for they were

---

* *Stanitsa*—a Cossack settlement.—*Trans.*

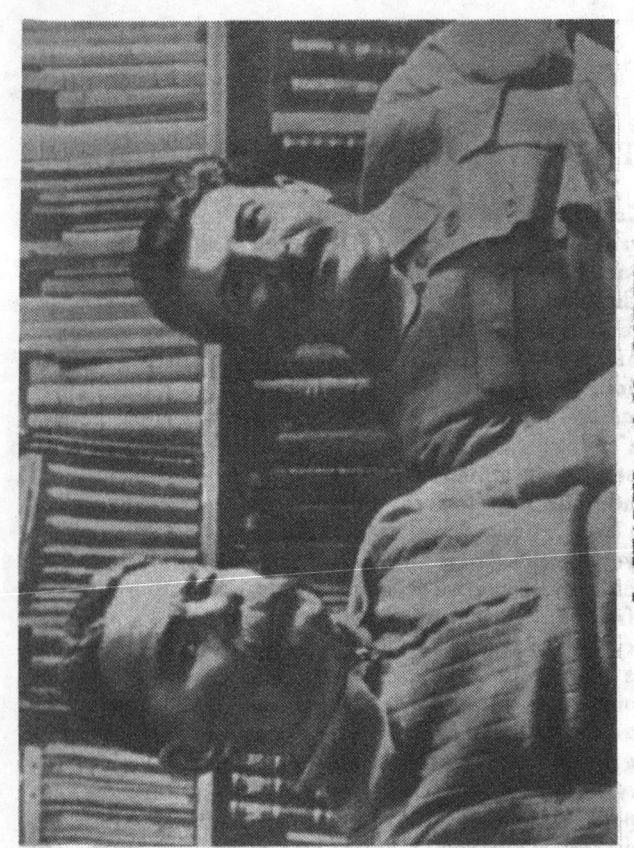

J. STALIN and M. GORKY
Moscow—1936

sure to be loaded with silks from Persia or Eastern sweetmeats. Afrikan sold the stolen property and with the proceeds organized drunken orgies which he forced Gorky to join in.

But Gorky, fortunately, only served for a few months at this station. He made an enemy of Afrikan's cook, an enormous woman who was as huge as her employer. She was forever threatening Gorky:

"I'll make you smart, my lad!"

And after Gorky had been on duty all night, she would make him do jobs about the house—sweep the yard, tend the fires and clean the stable.

Gorky sent a complaint to the head office of the railway. Nobody at the head office, of course, would have taken the trouble to consider a complaint lodged by a night watchman against some cook or other. But Gorky hit on the idea of drawing up his statement in the form of a poem. The bored railway officials read the unusual document and decided to make things easier for Gorky. He was transferred to the goods station at Borisoglebsk and set to watch sacks and tarpaulins.

Life in this provincial town astounded Gorky by the grotesque and senseless forms it took.

The mayor of the town would order divine services to be held in order to exorcise the devils in some well or other; the teacher of the local school beat his wife every Saturday in the public bathhouse. And neither the prayers nor the floggings gave rise to the least indignation or surprise in Borisoglebsk. . . .

Gorky tells about his life in Borisoglebsk in his story *The Watchman*:

"Dreaming as ever of performing some deed of glory, of the radiant joys of life, I kept watch over sacks and tarpaulins, stacks of snow fences, sleepers and wood, guarding them from the Cossacks of the near-by *stanitsa*. I read Heine and Shakespeare, but sometimes of a night I would suddenly come back to earth with

a start, to the dry rot that was pervading everything around me, and I would sit or lie for hours, my mind utterly blank, as though stunned by a blow on the head."

A good many educated people served on the railway at Borisoglebsk—former university or college students, economists and army officers. Some of them were considered to be politically "unreliable," and had been either in prison or in exile.

Burning with indignation, Gorky told them what he thought of the Borisoglebsk philistines. But they merely laughed. All these stories of his seemed nothing but funny anecdotes to them.

Gorky was surprised at this attitude. When he was in Kazan, in the revolutionary circles there, he had felt that some invisible barrier separated him from the intellectuals. This had caused him many a heartache, but, nevertheless, he had respected them. Here, in Borisoglebsk, he saw in the intellectuals nothing but vulgar, narrow-minded snobs.

Only one of them, a man by the name of Bazhenov, after hearing Gorky out, said:

"It's simply dreadful!"

He said this in all sincerity and Gorky felt a respect for the man.

Gorky was steeped with morbid impressions, as it were. He became subject to strange fits of anger and contempt for people. The books he read during this period of bitter loneliness told him that life was not only foul and stupid but that it also had its bright and happy side.

Gorky firmly believed this. But what life had in store for him was yet another heartache.

From Borisoglebsk Gorky was transferred to Krutaya railway station as a check weighman.

At this tiny station lost in the steppe a man felt as though he had been placed under some huge invisible bell jar—one's heart contracted so with a feeling of desolation. Marmots whistled, mosquitoes whined, an occasional train would rumble past, and this was all. At Borisoglebsk there had at least been books and after he had finished with his sacks and tarpaulins Gorky would remain alone with Heine or Shakespeare. But here there was nothing barring a few dog-eared back numbers of *Neva*.

One day Gorky received intimation at Krutaya that his only friend at Borisoglebsk, Bazhenov, had shot himself in the churchyard. In a farewell letter he had requested that all his books be sent to Krutaya, to "Maximich...."

Many a time had Gorky witnessed how the people who made away with themselves were just those people who, in his opinion, were better than the others....

* * *

Gorky was getting on for twenty-two. The time was nearing for him to report for military service.

He left Krutaya and set out on foot for Nizhni-Novgorod.

It was then spring, but not before autumn did Gorky hope to reach his native town.

Chapter IV

"THE SONG OF THE OLD OAK"

He tramped through the Don country, visited the Tambov and Ryazan Regions, stopped at *stanitsas*, villages, monasteries, earning enough to keep himself going by doing chance jobs on the road.

This was Gorky's first journey through Russia.

Finally, in September, he reached Moscow.

He hastened to the Khamovniki district—to the old manor house in which Tolstoy lived.

Gorky did not find Tolstoy at home. Sofia Andreyevna, the wife of the great writer, invited the stranger into the kitchen and treated him to coffee and rolls. The Countess remarked that a lot of shady ne'er-do-wells were always coming to see Lev Nikolayevich. Gorky politely agreed with her.

Gorky had to go on further, to Nizhni-Novgorod. This was how he recalled this lap of his journey.

"It was the end of September. The earth was being generously showered by the autumn rains. A cold wind swept the stubble-covered fields, the woods were ablaze with colour; it was the most beautiful season of the year, but hardly the best time for travelling on foot and particularly in torn shoes.

"At the Moscow goods station, I persuaded a railway guard to give me a lift in a cattle van in which eight Cherkess bulls were being consigned to the slaughter house at Nizhni-Novgorod. Five of them were more or less well-behaved but the rest did not like my looks for some reason or other and did their best all the way to make things unpleasant for me. Whenever they succeeded they would snort and bellow with satisfaction.

"The railway guard, an undersized, bandy-legged sot with nibbled whiskers foisted the job of feeding my travelling companions on to me; at every stop he would shove an armful of hay through the door and order me:

"Feed 'em!"

"I spent thirty-four hours in the company of these bulls, naively reflecting all the time that never again in my life would I ever meet with such uncouth brutes as they were."

Gorky did not go to Nizhni-Novgorod empty-handed. In his knapsack he had a notebook full of verse and a poem entitled: *The Song of the Old Oak*.

Gorky was delighted with this poem. He was firmly convinced that once published it would undoubtedly leave an indelible impression on the minds of his fellow men.

Gorky was not accepted into the army.

"He's no good, his lung's punctured," was the verdict of the military surgeon.

He had to find something to do. And so this ex-dishwasher, pretzel-maker, stage-super and railway night watchman became an unskilled labourer in a brewery. Amongst his other duties was delivering "Bavarian kvas" to customers. . . .

People in the street would turn to look at him, at his strange rig-out—the wide-brimmed hat of an opera bandit, a white cook's tunic and the blue trousers of a police officer.

Gorky also attracted the attention of the police. But what aroused their interest was not the quaint outfit of the "Bavarian kvas" deliveryman but something quite different. . . .

Many revolutionaries happened to live in Nizhni-Novgorod at the time. Amongst them were some old friends of Gorky's from Kazan, people who had been banished to Nizhni-Novgorod after the disturbances in the Kazan University.

The man in the cook's tunic and policeman's trousers began to frequent meetings of the illegal circles.

Gorky took lodgings together with two other political exiles from Kazan—a former teacher by the name of Chekhin and an ex-student called Somov.

This, in particular, aroused the suspicions of the authorities.

Police spies began to watch the house where Gorky and his comrades lived.

Inquiries were sent out to various towns asking for information about the Nizhni-Novgorod artisan Alexei Peshkov.

Before long a warrant for Somov's arrest was received from St. Petersburg.

The police, however, were too late. Somov had already disappeared. They questioned Gorky.

"Peshkov conducted himself under cross-examination in a brazen, highly insolent manner," the gendarmes reported to their chief.

Gorky was arrested and detained in one of the four circular towers of the Nizhni-Novgorod prison.

"What kind of a revolutionary do you think you are?" the gendarme general remarked irritably to him during the interrogation. "You write poems and the like.... Now when I let you out you'd better show that stuff of yours to Korolenko. Do you know him?"

And at parting he added:

"What you should do is study, well, h'm, write, but not this sort of things...."

By "this sort of things" he meant: revolutionary activity. The general could not have foreseen that in a few years time it would be precisely Gorky's writings that would give him and his men so much trouble.

Gorky was detained in the prison for a month. Then he was set free. But he was already listed as an "unreliable" and kept under constant surveillance by the police.

Gorky did not give up the revolutionary struggle. But in one respect he did follow the advice of the gendarme general, he went to see Korolenko.

Vladimir Korolenko, who lived in Nizhni-Novgorod at the time, was widely known all over the country. His stories and novels were very popular amongst the intelligentsia, while government officials and the merchant class stood in dread of his scathing articles in the press.

A strange legend was current amongst the people at large that Korolenko had been sent by somebody from abroad to fight against the tsarist government. . . .

Stern-faced and clumsy, Gorky placed before Korolenko his poem, *The Song of the Old Oak*, the poem of which he was so proud.

Korolenko turned over the leaves of the bulky manuscript.

"Here you write 'zizgag,' " he said. "That's only a slip of the pen, of course. There is no such word. It should be—'zigzag'. . . ."

Gorky was grateful to the well-known writer, for the way he spared the self-esteem of a budding author. But, alas, "zizgag" was no slip of the pen. . . .

Korolenko went on to discuss the merits of Gorky's literary attempt. He said that it lacked consonance.

The poem contained the following passage:

"I have come into the world not to compromise. And since that's so. . . ."

" 'And since that's so'—no, it's no good!" Korolenko remarked. "It's a clumsy and inelegant turn of speech. And since that's so, since it's so—can you hear the way it sounds?"

Gorky noticed it for the first time.

Several days later Korolenko returned the manuscript. On the cover he had written:

"It is hard to form an opinion of what you are capable of from this 'Song' but I think you have talent. Write something about what you have experienced yourself and show it to me. I am no judge of verse and found yours hard to understand although some of the lines are vivid and forceful."

Never again—neither poems nor prose—Gorky decided.

Gorky was earnest in his resolve not to write. During the two years he lived in Nizhni-Novgorod he never once took up his pen.

Yet he needed some other interest in life, apart from rolling beer barrels about in a brewery.

But things shaped themselves in such a way that here, in Nizhni-Novgorod, Gorky once again began to feel the old, familiar void, reminding him of the dreary days of his life at Krutaya.

He attended the study circles of the intellectuals. Here he met many excellent people. But Gorky was coming to realize ever more clearly that even the best of them were detached from the people and from life. They read books, argued glibly and skilfully—and that was all.

Gorky, however, was searching for something else—he was searching for real life and real emotions. . . .

He came to the conclusion that the best thing he could do would be to go away somewhere, on a long journey. He tried to sign on as a volunteer with a topographical expedition. An officer he knew promised to take him to the Pamirs.

But Gorky did not go with the expedition—he was rejected as an "unreliable."

One summer night found Gorky sitting on a bench on the Cliff; from where he sat he had a view of the Volga and the mist-shrouded meadows beyond the rivers.

A stranger with a curly beard silently took a seat beside him.

The stranger was Korolenko.

"Well," he asked, "are you writing?"

"No."

"It's a pity. I am seriously inclined to believe that you have talent. You are in a bad mood, sir."

This was true: Gorky was in a bad mood. He had lost his faith in his literary talent, the academic debates of the intellectuals only bored him and seemed futile, and last but not least he was in love. He was passionately in love for the first time, but the woman he loved was married and hesitated to leave her husband for his sake. . . .

Gorky left Nizhni-Novgorod, just as two years before he had left the wayside railway station, to wander once again through Russia.

Chapter V
WANDERINGS

> "He is a highly suspicious character—well read, wields a good pen and has covered practically the whole of Russia (mostly on foot)."
>
> (*From the police files re: Gorky*)

Gorky followed the Volga. At Tsaritsyn he left the river and struck across country over the steppe.

For a time he lived in Rostov. There was work to be had in the filthy port there—unloading damp hides and crates of tobacco from a Turkish steamer. The working day was almost as long as at Semyonov's bakery, fifteen hours a day. But here at least Gorky received fifty kopecks for a day's work.

This was untold wealth. Semyonov had only paid him ten kopecks.

In the brief intervals between work Gorky and his new comrades would make a dash for one of the jerry-built tripe kitchens on the bank. On days when he did particularly well he would go to a tavern with the enigmatic name of "Yeishop," which was always crowded with longshoremen and carters.

Gorky lived in a basement near the port. An old woman rented him a corner of her room for five kopecks a night.

Then he left Rostov, tramped through the Ukraine, and from there wandered on to Bessarabia, to the banks of the Danube, to the very border of Rumania.

Several years later the police wrote in a report to the authorities at St. Petersburg:

"Peshkov made his way on foot from Nizhni-Novgorod to Bessarabia with the object of getting to Rumania and ultimately to France, but since he was not allowed to cross the frontier he turned back towards the Crimea and Transcaucasia."

On his way back from Bessarabia to the Transcaucasus—an enormous distance of several thousand versts—Gorky kept more or less closely to the coastline of the Black Sea.

He wandered on for a long time, for almost two years.

He tramped from village to village, from *aul* to *aul*, discovering ever new and strange lands: Moldavia and the Crimea, the Kuban and Georgia.

A multitude of things were impressed on his mind—the sea, ports, ships, herds of horses, campfires in the wide open steppes, mountain ranges hazy in the distance, gypsy camps, Tatar shepherds, monks, smugglers, fishermen, vagabonds, pilgrims. . . .

He was nearly drowned in the Kerch Straits. He was snowbound during a blizzard on the Georgian Military Highway. . . .

And as always hunger dogged his steps.

He walked through a land of plenty but often enough he did not have even a crust of bread in his knapsack; he considered it a crime but, worst of all, it hindered him from thinking.

It was good in Abkhazia. Here Gorky lived mostly on wild honey. The bees gathered the honey from the laurel and azalea flowers; he would look for it in the hollows of trees and fill his billycan.

But when things went hard with him Gorky would be ready to tackle any job. He worked at various times as a farmhand in the Cherkessian villages in the Caucasus, and for Jewish colonists in the Ukraine, as a cook, a labourer in a salt pit and a navvy on a road construction job. In fishing villages he earned his supper by helping to haul in the net.

On one occasion he was driven to reading prayers over a dead body—there was no other work to be had in that particular village. And so he read prayers all night long and, in the morning, taking a hunk of bread and refusing the money offered him, he set out once more on his journey across the steppe.

What drove him on? He often wondered himself.

It was wonderful to watch a Turkish felucca heading slowly out to sea, to listen to the field mice rustling in the steppe grass, to see leaves twisting and turning on the foam-flecked surface of some turbulent mountain stream, to recognize the tapping of a woodpecker on a hornbeam....

But far more wonderful and important was to wander over every road, and to meet people and strive to understand them.

Before leaving Nizhni-Novgorod Gorky had read all of Pomyalovski's works—a writer of whom he was very fond.

In one of his novels Pomyalovski had stated that one must study human nature in every walk of life—shopkeepers and vagabonds, firemen and tramps....

And Gorky closely observed men and women in these and other walks of life, studied the people of whom some of his mentors had talked so much and known so little.

But often from a mere observer he became a participant in events, particularly if these events stung him to the quick, making his blood boil with indignation.

In one Ukrainian village he happened to witness what was known locally as a "trotting" ordeal—a drastic punishment meted out to a woman accused of being unfaithful to her husband.

A frail little woman, little more than a girl, was harnessed stark naked to a cart, together with a horse. A muzhik with a shock of sandy hair and blood-shot eyes, the woman's husband, climbed into the cart and drove off, lashing the harnessed pair with a whip, which he brought down in turn first on the horse's back and then on his wife's naked body.

And behind the cart followed a hooting, jeering mob....

For the villagers this was no brutal reprisal but an ordinary custom, a commonplace incident and nothing more.

Nobody considered that what the sandy-headed muzhik was doing was something savage, while the thought of taking the unfortunate woman's part never so much as entered their heads.

Gorky later on described this incident in his story *The Trotting Ordeal*, concluding his narrative with the words:

"I saw this with my own eyes in 1891, on July 15, in the village of Kandibovka, Kherson Gubernia, Nikolayev Uyezd."

He did not mention, however, that there was one man who did make an attempt to stand up for the poor woman and that that man was the author himself—Gorky.

He pitted himself against the mob. All the fury of the villagers turned against the stranger. They beat him up even more cruelly than the woman, ran him out of the village and left him lying in the mud by the roadside.

Gorky lay there unconscious.

An organ grinder who happened to be passing by on his way from some village fair noticed a blood-stained man lying in the bushes, put him into his cart and took him to the hospital at Nikolayev. Gorky was detained in hospital a long time—the villagers of Kandibovka had almost beaten the life out of him.

It was only by accident that Gorky had witnessed the tragic incident at Kandibovka. But quite often during his wanderings he suddenly turned off the road to follow some country track in order to see for himself how the people lived in the farms and villages.

Passing through the Kuban *stanitsas* he heard that a "rinderpest riot" had taken place in the town of Maikop. The local inhabitants, incensed by the inept measures of the tsarist officials in combating the cattle plague, had beaten up the government veterinary surgeons.

The local authorities had called out the troops. The Cossacks had opened fire on a crowd of peasants, many of whom had been killed.

Gorky hastened to Maikop.

When he got there he found widows in tears, an atmosphere of universal terror and the Cossacks riding roughshod through the streets.

The newcomer immediately attracted the attention of the authorities. Gorky was arrested and confined in the army barracks—there was no more room left in the local prison.

During the interrogation a heavily whiskered colonel of the gendarmes tried to ascertain what business had brought Gorky to Maikop in such troublous times.

"I want to know Russia," Gorky replied briefly.

The colonel rapped out an oath:

"This is not Russia but a piggery!"

Everything about the arrested man, who gave his name as Peshkov, aroused the suspicions of the police. He was tramping about the country without any definite occupation, had books in his knapsack and even a notebook of verse, and during the interrogation answered insolently, with a look of contempt in his eyes.

But there was no direct evidence on which to charge the prisoner. He was kept under lock and key at the barracks for a few days and then released.

The Maikop barracks was Gorky's second prison in his chequered career.

Chapter VI

THE FIRST STORY

Gorky's long ramblings through the South of Russia finally came to an end in the Caucasus, in Tiflis.

But here, too, life was no bed of roses: the same old drudgery, a basement for a lodging, clashes with the police, back-breaking work.... Nevertheless these were good days, perhaps the best in young Gorky's life.

In Tiflis Gorky met new people and made new friends.

He started work in the railway repair shops and before long got in touch with revolutionary-minded worker and students. And in them Gorky found not condescending mentors but plain and good comrades.

Together with them he carried on revolutionary propaganda among the workers, mainly among the railwaymen, and lived in constant expectation of a visit from the "brass buttons," as they dubbed the gendarmes.

Time and again Gorky was seized with the wanderlust. At one time he thought of becoming a strolling actor—to wander up and down the country with a knapsack on his back and stage simple shows in the villages. He even got together a small troupe....

But Gorky did not become a strolling actor. In Tiflis he met a man who sensed his latent talent and his true vocation.

The man in question was Alexander Mefodievich Kaluzhni.

Alexander Kaluzhni was a member of a secret society known as the "Narodnaya Volya," and had already served a term of six years in prison for his revolutionary activities. He possessed what was probably the rarest of all talents—the talent of being human. He knew how to dispose people to himself. He was a good listener and a good judge of character, and knew how to draw out the best in people and help them to cultivate this best themselves.

In his first meetings with Kaluzhni Gorky told him about his wanderings through Bessarabia and along the Volga, about his adventures on the road and about himself. Looking silently at his companion, Kaluzhni saw that he was not merely a husky young fellow with an uncommon destiny, an aimless tramp with a whimsical turn of mind and a grim look on his face.

In Gorky's stories Kaluzhni sensed a great talent and a magnanimous heart.

This chance acquaintanceship developed into a deep, sincere friendship.

Kaluzhni saw that Gorky would make a mark for himself in literature.

"Write about all this," he repeated insistently, fascinated by the narratives of his new friend.

Gorky did write, but not what Kaluzhni expected of him.

By this time Gorky had accumulated a boundless store of rich impressions. Life had thrown him together with people in basements, workshops and ships' cabins, in peasants' log huts and in snug little urban houses, in barns and in watchman's huts. He knew what it meant to be a ragpicker, cook, iconpainter, pretzel-maker, stevedore, peddler and railwayman. He had seen his country as only a wayfarer could see it—from brook to brook, from campfire to campfire. . . .

And all he had to do, it seemed, was write about this, about himself, about what he had seen with his own eyes, his own reflections. But when Gorky took up the pen all this wealth of impressions somehow faded from his memory and other words, words from books he had read of late came into his mind. And Gorky wrote words that were not his own, imitating Byron's poems or the verse of the Italian poet Leopardi.

The result was something noisy but tinny.

Kaluzhni understood all this.

"Write only of what you've seen yourself," he urged Gorky.

Recalling one day his wanderings through Bessarabia, Gorky related the legend of Radda and Loyko Zobar which he had heard in a gypsy camp from an old gypsy by the name of Makar Chudra.

The legend held everybody spellbound. Gorky decided to write up his meeting with the old gypsy in the form of a story.

Kaluzhni took the narrative to the editor of the *Kavkas*, an important Tiflis newspaper.

The story took the editor's fancy. Only one thing was lacking in the MS—the signature. The author coined it there and then, while sitting in the editorial office of the newspaper.

"Maxim Gorky...."*

In September 1892 *Makar Chudra*—Gorky's first story appeared in print.

Late in the autumn Gorky set out on his way back to his native town, to Nizhni-Novgorod.

From Tiflis Gorky carried away with him a life-long memory of Kaluzhni—the man who first discovered the writer in him.

---

* Maxim Gorky — Maxim Bitter. — *Trans.*

V. I. LENIN and M. GORKY
Petrograd—1920

Chapter VII

YEGUDIL KHLAMIDA

Gorky did not return alone. Olga, the woman he had fallen in love with in Nizhni-Novgorod and whose image had accompanied him throughout his long wanderings, had proved to be in Tiflis.

When Gorky had accidentally heard of this, he had fainted—for the first time in his life.

Olga, it appeared, had left her husband and now there was no reason why they should not live together. She accompanied Gorky back to Nizhni-Novgorod.

They rented an old bathhouse in the garden of a tipsy priest and set up house. Winter came. It was bitterly cold in the bathhouse and, when they heated it, the place reeked of soap and birch twigs.*

Gorky worked as a clerk in the office of a well-known Nizhni-Novgorod liberal lawyer by the name of Lanin. He copied out applications and appeals and attended court on Lanin's business, but at night, sitting in the outroom which served him as a study, he read Balzac and the philosophers and dreamed of travelling to distant lands—to India, and Ceylon. But most often he wrote stories.

He hesitated to send them to a publishers. Literature to him was a lofty calling, verging almost on the marvellous; his own efforts seemed dull and poor.

---

* In the Russian steambaths the people slap themselves with birch twigs in order to stimulate their circulation.—*Trans.*

One day Gorky wrote a story of how he and a companion named Emelian Pilai had tramped hungrily along the coast of the Black Sea; at night, in the open steppe, his friend had told him of how he had made an unlucky attempt to "bash a moneybag over the head...."

A friend of Gorky's took the manuscript to Moscow and shortly after he saw his *Emelian Pilai* published in the *Russkiye Vedomosti*. This decided Gorky on his next step. He sent his stories to Kazan, to the editor of the *Volzhsky Vestnik*.

Gorky received a cheque for something like thirty roubles from Kazan. It seemed like a small fortune to him.

Korolenko was struck by Gorky's stories. He wanted to meet this young writer who signed his stories with the strange pen name of Maxim Gorky.

Gorky called at the wooden house on the outskirts of the city. And in Maxim Gorky Korolenko recognized the unknown young man who several years ago had brought him a poem about an old oak.... In a tiny room filled with flowers, books and newspaper files, the two men discussed literature, the Russian countryside and those lonely Russians whom poverty and restlessness were driving over the numerous roads of the country.

Korolenko praised Gorky's stories.

"You have a very marked personal style," he said. "Not everything is just pat, it wants a little extra polish, but it's interesting for all that."

"So you think I will be able to write?" Gorky asked.

"Of course!" Korolenko exclaimed, somewhat surprised. "You are writing already—and being published, so what more do you want? If you need advice, bring your manuscripts round...."

In Korolenko, a great and truthful artist, Gorky found an attentive and painstaking teacher.

Korolenko's remarks were simple but necessary and to the point. He advised Gorky not to let himself be carried away by beautifully sounding phrases, to be sparing in his use of words and not to idealize people.

And lastly he gave Gorky a piece of friendly advice—to leave Nizhni-Novgorod. Korolenko had heard of Gorky's straitened circumstances, of his incongruous existence in the one-time bathhouse and of the fact that the young writer's domestic life was none too happy. . . .

Gorky himself realized that things could not go on much longer in the same way and that perhaps the best course would be for him and Olga to part. He loved Olga but she was empty and frivolous and they lived in worlds apart. She was entirely indifferent to his literary strivings, his favourite books and the dreams he cherished so. . . .

Olga and he parted forever.

Korolenko invited Gorky to work on the staff of the *Samarskaya Gazeta*. Gorky accepted the proposal. The drudgery of copying out legal documents and affixing stamps, the incessant war he waged on the woodlice in the tiny bathhouse and the struggle for an extra penny to make both ends meet—all these suddenly became things of the past.

* * *

It was in Samara that Gorky's career became determined once and for all. Although some of his stories had already been published he had not been a writer in the literal sense of the word but a man of odd jobs, a clerk in a lawyer's office, with a precarious income. In Samara Gorky took up writing as a profession.

Besides Korolenko other well-known writers such as Mamin-Sibiryak, the author of *Alenushka's Tales*, and Garin-Mikhailovsky, the author of *The Childhood of Tyoma*, published their work in the *Samarskaya Gazeta*. And now Gorky's name appeared in the columns of the paper side by side with theirs. Every Sunday the readers of the *Samarskaya Gazeta* found a new story by Gorky.

Gorky recalled his recent past—the years of arduous toil, adventures, wanderings, fascinating encounters, and it was from this variegated, rich, inexhaustible store of his memory that he drew the material for his stories—*The Trotting Ordeal*, *A Matter of Clasps*, and *Once in the Autumn*.

Gorky also wrote feuilletons for the *Samarskaya Gazeta* on subjects dealing with local life.

He wrote about the tramcar service and the municipal park, the local hooligans and the summer theatre, the hospital and the town council. The feuilletons were ruthless and bitter. Gorky signed them with the strange name of "Yegudil Khlamida."

"You're not much of a feuilleton writer," Garin-Mikhailovsky told him bluntly when they were introduced to each other. "You have a sense of humour, of the rough and ready kind, but you don't know how to use it to advantage."

Gorky was well aware that "Yegudil Khlamida" wrote clumsily and called his work as a feature writer "that darned job."

And yet, weak as "Yegudil Khlamida's" articles were, in comparison with Maxim Gorky's stories, they served their purpose. "Khlamida's" feuilletons very often pilloried the powers that be in Samara—the wealthy grain and cattle dealers. In his rough and ready way "Khlamida" was ever ready to take up the cudgels in defence of the working-class youth, servants, the poor, in defence of those people whose conditions in life were near and comprehensible to him.

Gorky lived a secluded life in Samara, in a small cottage overlooking the Volga. He knew that he had a lot of hard work ahead of him and he worked as only a man can who after a long period of groping has at last found his true vocation.

When Gorky first came to Samara "zizgags" and similar slips of the pen would once in a while still creep into his manuscripts. But he already had a good knowledge of Shakespeare and Goethe, Dickens and Maupassant, Thackeray and Hugo, knew Lermontov's and Baratinsky's poems by heart and always carried a volume of Flaubert or Stendhal about with him—French writers who had not yet found recognition at the time in Russia.

But in time the spelling mistakes disappeared, while Gorky's style became more and more confident. For days at a stretch he would work on a manuscript or read in his room, which was unfurnished save for an iron campbed, shelves stocked with books and a deal table piled high with papers. The day was not long enough for him and he worked far into the night.

Belated passers-by in the deserted Voznesensky Street who chanced to glance in at the window of Gorky's basement would see in the yellow glare of a paraffin lamp a man's head bent over the loose sheets of a manuscript, his hair falling in unruly strands over his face.

Dawn would come, the shaft of light from the lamp would pale in the rising sun, but the lamp would still go on burning.

* * *

When Gorky had first come to Samara, the local journalists had known of only one Peshkov, a certain Cossack officer who had won fame by riding on horseback from Siberia to St. Petersburg. The editors of *Samarskaya Gazeta* had had to explain that the Peshkov who had been invited on the staff of their paper was "not an officer but a *bosyak.*"

A year later Gorky had already made a name for himself. All the Volga newspapers tried to get the young writer to join their staffs. He also received an invitation from the *Nizhnegorodski Listok*.

And so Gorky returned once again to Nizhni-Novgorod.

Chapter VIII

FAME

Gorky found Nizhni-Novgorod changed. The old familiar smells of axle grease, sour cabbage and dried fish now mingled with those of fresh paint and boiling tar. On every hand houses were being decorated and sidewalks paved.

An All-Russian Industrial Exhibition was due to be opened in the town. The country was passing through an industrial boom. The purpose of the exhibition was to demonstrate to the whole of Europe the achievements and might of Russian capital.

In the middle of a bleak wasteland adjoining a squalid slum pavilions sprung up which resembled birthday cakes, fantastically gabled cottages, and overturned troughs. The pavilions were stocked with cotton goods, hemp ropes, icons, gaily coloured porcelains, golden brocades, forks, moroccos. . . . Shepherds from Vladimir Gubernia, brought especially for the exhibition, blew blasts on ram's horns, while a red-headed man in Russian national costume made the bells peal to the tune of "Glory, Glory Our Russian Tsar." A double-headed golden eagle glittered over the exhibition and above it all was moored a captive grey balloon.

Nicholas II arrived to open the exhibition. The merchants paid homage to His Majesty with wax candles, coloured bottles and Kazan soap. A chapel was built out of the candles, a triumphal arch out of bottles, and busts of the Romanoffs were fashioned out of the soap.

It was a solemn display of the country's wealth and the stupidity of its rulers. A homemade piano was on exhibition, the chords of which were made of ox tendons instead of wire. The instrument rattled and clattered like an old, broken down stage coach. One brilliant inventor exhibited a machine which in his own humble opinion was to create a mighty revolution in engineering. The machine turned out to be an antediluvian bicycle. An ex-notary displayed to the public a gadget of his own design with which to swat gadflies on horses; but the horses treated with the instrument were almost driven crazy. Visitors were shown a live walrus, forks manufactured by the Pavlov handicraftsmen and porcelain accessories for lavatories; but a canvas by the famous Russian painter Vrubel was not admitted for exhibition.

Visitors to the exhibition were given an opportunity to go up on the captive balloon.

"We thank you heartily," replied an old man with a sharp pointed beard, a petty tradesman by his looks, voicing the sentiments of everybody present. "But supposing," he went on enquiringly, "you let the bladder go, can it fly up to God? It can't, you say? Then what in the name of the devil do we want to go gallivanting about in the sky for?"

The columns of the papers were filled with accounts of the exhibition. The elaborate fretwork of the gabled cottages, the Vladimir shepherds and Pavlov forks— all this in the opinion of the newspaper correspondents spoke of the might and power of the Russian Empire.

Gorky, too, published a series of articles on the exhibition.

Now he no longer wrote about the Samara tram service, or the municipal park, but on subjects that were riveting the attention of the whole country.

Gorky's articles were a stern indictment.

Describing the pavilions in which oil, gold, leather and soap were exhibited he spoke of the conditions of life of the people who extracted the oil, washed the gold, tanned the hides and manufactured the soap.

Gorky knew many things about their lives from his own experience and in his articles he drew a faithful picture for the benefit of his readers.

It was about this time, too, that *In the Steppe*, *Konovalov* and *Creatures that Once Were Men* appeared. In publishing these stories about *bosyaks* and vagrants at a time when the Nizhni-Novgorod festivities were in full swing the author was in fact broadly hinting to the people who flocked to the pavilion halls that not far away were "creatures that once were men," and that the blame for this lay at the door of the rulers of Russia.

* * *

Gorky fell sick about this time. His hungry, poverty-stricken youth, his life as a homeless waif coupled with years of hard physical labour and the bullet from the Tula revolver and now, finally, his intense work as a writer could not but tell on him.

Gorky fought to overcome what he termed his "touch of T. B." and went on writing. But his health grew steadily worse. Many of his friends were under the impression that he would never recover. The doctors ordered him to go South. He lived for a while in the Crimea and then in the Ukraine, in the quiet little village of Manuilovka.

Gorky felt comfortable at Manuilovka. Everything pleased him there—the large park, the family of owls in the old linden tree, the river teeming with enormous pike, the bells chiming the hour at night.

The Crimea and Manuilovka set Gorky on his feet. He returned to Nizhni-Novgorod—to life and work.

Gorky collected his tales and narratives into two small volumes. After many difficulties he at last found a publishing house willing to risk printing the books of an author whose work so far had appeared only in the provincial press.

The two modest little volumes finally appeared and almost overnight the whole of reading Russia began to speak of this new star on the literary horizon. Gorky's books sold like hot cakes, in tens of thousands of copies.

Gorky's stories laid bare the bitter and stubborn truth of contemporary Russian life. He held nothing back. And this truth was uttered not by a weak, impotent, despairing littérateur. Every line he wrote was permeated with his unconquerable faith in man. The reader was impressed by the strength and vitality of the stories of this newcomer to the field of literature.

Gorky's first books brought him real fame.

The name of the new writer took its place alongside those of his great contemporaries—Leo Tolstoy and Anton Chekhov.

Chapter IX

METEKH CASTLE AND THE NIZHNI-NOVGOROD GAOL

> "The double-headed eagle of the autocracy was not merely the coat of arms of the Empire but an exceedingly live and actively pernicious bird."
>
> *(Gorky: Talks on Craftsmanship)*

Gorky's fame as a writer grew by leaps and bounds and became a source of growing anxiety to the tsarist government.

The authorities realized that they had an implacable enemy in Gorky. An open war flared up between the government and the young writer, a war that went on incessantly for twenty long years.

A revolutionary worker by the name of Afanasyev was arrested in Tiflis When the police searched his rooms they found a photograph with the inscription: "To dear Fedya Afanasyev. In remembrance of Maximich."

The gendarmes succeeded in ascertaining who Maximich was.

Gorky was arrested in Nizhni-Novgorod and sent to Tiflis, where he was confined in Metekh Castle—the gaol usually reserved for political prisoners.

He paced the cell wondering why he had been incarcerated in this particular prison. The window looked out on the grey embattled prison walls, the muddy waters of the River Kura and the wooden balconied houses on the bank. . . .

The warder paced up and down the corridor rattling his keys. Whenever he lost his temper he would shout at Gorky:

"May you rot here for another ten years!"

Had the gendarmes succeeded in implicating Gorky in the Afanasyev case, the warder's wishes might have come true and Gorky would have had to serve a long stretch in Metekh Castle, but fortunately for him they could not find anything incriminating.

Gorky returned to Nizhni-Novgorod. From then on he was kept under close surveillance by the police. Strange individuals were always hovering around the two-storeyed wooden house in which he lived. One of them would be sitting on a bench, making believe that he was idly surveying the sky. Another would be leaning against a lamp post, ostensibly engrossed in the contents of a newspaper. The driver of the drozhky drawn up near the front door also behaved strangely: he would readily agree to take Gorky or any of his visitors wherever they pleased, free of charge if need be. But he would never take another fare. For the sky-gazer and newspaper reader and the drozhky driver were all detectives in disguise whose job it was to observe every step of the writer and his friends.

This was no easy task. Gorky always had hosts of visitors. People from all walks of life would be ushered into his study, which was hung with canvases by Vasnetsov and Levitan—actors, foremen, artists, foreigners touring the country, high-school girls, merchants. . . .

In one of his letters from Nizhni-Novgorod Gorky wrote:

"Crowds of different people come to see me every day. One asks for a book, another dabbles in verse. . . . A type-setter, just back from exile, comes to pay his respects; then the wife of a vice-governor brings a batch of illegal pamphlets, followed by a seamstress who will be shortly coming up for trial, and after the seamstress comes the general in command of the local artillery brigade with a request to organize theatricals for his men. Bugrov, the merchant, invites me to have a heart-to-heart talk on God while Schmelling, the president of the dramatic club—a hefty fellow who showed me out of the club last year for not being in a morning coat—requests me to remonstrate with the ladies who will not listen to him. I never refuse anybody. Through the good offices of the vice-governor's wife the type-setter will be taken on the staff of the Gubernia printshop where he will set about organizing a workers' circle. Bugrov, himself, will provide them with money for books. I am always perfectly willing to remonstrate with the ladies and in return for this they will help my seamstress start a cooperative dressmakers shop; I will fix up the theatricals for the general and he, in his turn, will let me have the use of the Riding School grounds at Christmas free of charge, not to mention a band."*

Gorky was planning a Christmas party for the poor children of Nizhni-Novgorod. He was anxious to give them a real holiday. His flat was stacked with cases and boxes containing presents for the youngsters. Everywhere were rolls of material which nimble fingers were busily making into shirts.

Gorky looked on happily at the preparations.

The Christmas tree was enormous, a mass of green illuminated with coloured electric lights.

Some five hundred children came—a whole army of grimy youngsters from the slums. A detachment of waifs from the Lower Market marched in—'The Gorky Detachment"—with a red banner at its head.

---

* From Gorky's letter to L. V. Sredin. Published here for the first time.—*Ed.*

Gorky watched the children with a sad look in his eyes.

"The poor little mites were so bewildered by the long rows of tables loaded with presents and at the sight of the Christmas tree, gorgeously decorated and ablaze with electric lights, that they circled round and round the hall in a dense, motley stream, coughing all the while in a special sort of way, sadly, pitifully, just like toil-worn old folks. They walked around silently, solemnly; but their eyes gleamed eagerly, such grave, serious eyes. It wasn't pleasant, you know.

"...When the poor things were handed out their presents—each one was given a cake, a bag of sweets (about a pound and a half), a pair of shoes, shirt, dress, blouse, cap, shawl—many of them, you know, burst into tears out of sheer joy, while others dashed off into a corner hugging their presents to their breasts, and still others squatted down on the floor there and then and began to eat."

Gorky, also, hit on another idea: pictures of all kinds were cut out of the illustrated magazines and made into albums for the village children.

"They never see anything," Gorky said. "And here they'll see towns and rivers and distant lands.... They will see splendid people and will want to know what they have done. You see?..."

Nor did Gorky forget the grown-ups, the people who were usually referred to as *bosyaks*.

In a spacious pillared building which was known all over the city as Column House, Gorky organized a daytime shelter for the unemployed and homeless. There was a library and a piano there, and the *bosyaks* who visited Column House felt as if they were human beings again.

But it was not the Christmas tree or the albums or even Column House which induced the police to keep a still closer watch on Gorky's movements. He began to make frequent visits to Sormovo—the working-class district of Nizhni-Novgorod, where the large works and plants were located.

Here, at secret meetings, people gathered to read the Social-Democratic newspaper *Iskra*, to which Lenin contributed. The newspaper was printed on thin rice-paper so that it could easily be swallowed in the event of a police raid. . . .

The Sormovo workers were among Gorky's frequent visitors. They came to him for advice, books and funds, with all of which Gorky supplied them freely.

In 1901 Gorky left on a visit to St. Petersburg. During his stay in the capital he saw the police brutally smash up a revolutionary student demonstration. He retaliated with a bold article attacking the Government, which was to blame for the outrage. And in his *Song of the Stormy Petrel*, which he wrote under the impressions of this incident, Gorky exclaimed:

"The storm! Soon the storm will break!"

The lines of this song were repeated all over the country.

On his way back from St. Petersburg Gorky succeeded in smuggling a mimeograph through to his friends in Nizhni-Novgorod—a duplicating machine which served the revolutionaries in lieu of a printing press. . . .

The *Okhranka*—the secret police—somehow got wind of the mimeograph.

Gorky was arrested on a charge of sedition and confined in the Nizhni-Novgorod prison, in tower No. 4 where, in spite of his ill health, he was subjected to a special regime as a dangerous criminal. All his correspondence was intercepted.

Gorky's arrest and imprisonment aroused widespread indignation. A wave of protest swept through the whole of Russia. Tolstoy came out in defence of the sick writer.

The government was forced to yield to public opinion. Gorky was released from prison and confined instead in his own home. Policemen were posted in his hall and in the kitchen. One of them would constantly intrude into his study and try to enter into a discussion with him.

Gorky settled down to his work again, often writing until late at night. This, more than anything else, aroused the suspicions of the police.

"He is always active, even during the night," they reported.

One day Gorky happened to meet the merchant Bugrov in the street.

"You're wasting your time!" he said heatedly to Gorky. "Your job is to record events, not to bring them to a head.... Only revolution will bring things to a head...."

Bugrov was not mistaken. Gorky was not only recording events but also helping to "bring them to a head." His contacts with the revolutionaries were becoming ever closer and he was rendering increasing assistance to the Sormovo workers.

The police and *Okhranka* agents were powerless to restrain him.

"His influence amongst the workers in general may express itself in a highly undesirable form," the Nizhni-Novgorod gendarmerie reported to St. Petersburg.

The government decided to banish Gorky from Nizhni-Novgorod, to put him somewhere out of reach of revolutionary Sormovo. He was ordered to go to Arzamas, a sleepy little town inhabited mostly by priests, narrow-minded townsfolk and retired civil servants.

The reprisals against Gorky evoked a wrathful protest from Lenin.

"One of Europe's foremost writers," wrote Lenin, "whose only weapon is freedom of speech, is being banished by the autocratic government without trial."

The term he had spent in prison had aggravated Gorky's illness. The doctors reported that his condition was extremely grave and required a course of treatment in the South. Pressure was brought to bear on the authorities by his numerous friends, including Tolstoy, as a result of which he received permission to spend a few months in the Crimea.

Gorky's send-off for the Crimea developed into a stormy demonstration. The railway station was crowded with students and workers long before his train was due to leave.

The crowd accompanied their favourite writer to his carriage with revolutionary songs.

The *Okhranka* gave orders for the train to be dispatched ahead of schedule. Two gendarmes were posted on the steps of the carriage....

The train pulled out of the station to the cries of: "Long live Maxim Gorky! Down with tyranny!"

* * *

Gorky was living in the Crimea when the notorious "Academy of Sciences incident" took place, an incident which served as an additional illustration of the extent to which Russian officialdom hated the author of the *Song of the Stormy Petrel*.

In 1902 the Academy of Sciences elected Gorky an honorary member. This act of homage to a man who had already been twice in prison aroused a storm of indignation in high government circles. The matter was reported to the Tsar. On a newspaper cutting reporting Gorky's election Nicholas II wrote the following remark:

"This goes beyond the bounds of originality."

And in a letter to the Minister of Education the Tsar wrote:

"... And this is the kind of man the Academy of Sciences is pleased to elect to its ranks in the present turbulent times. I am highly indignant at the whole affair."

This was enough for Gorky's election to be cancelled. The Academy of Sciences maintained a cowardly silence. Only two writers refused to be intimidated—Anton Chekhov and Vladimir Korolenko—who as a mark of protest against Gorky's expulsion from the Academy renounced their own titles of honorary members. This step on the part of Chekhov and Korolenko was a demonstration against the arbitrary action of the Tsar.

Chapter X

NIGHTINGALES AND SPIES

A certain Arzamas hairdresser styled himself "beard trimmer by appointment to the town."

And of the town itself he was wont to say:

"In some places there are floods, in others there are earthquakes, but in our parts—nothing ever happens! Take cholera—why we haven't even had that!"

There was a time when Arzamas seethed with revolt, when the people of Arzamas repudiated the authority of the tsar and flocked to the standards of Stepan Razin and Emelian Pugachov.

But the fiery Mordvinian and Chuvash Cossacks of those turbulent days had long ago rotted in their graves, the ancient Arzamas churchyard had long since become overgrown with weeds, while the revolts and executions of the past had long ago faded from memory. Arzamas had become a town of merchants and nuns, quiet, trustworthy, loyal. It traded in rabbit skins and lard, resounded to the pealing bells of five monasteries and thirty-six churches, listened to the croaking of frogs, read the *Yeparkhialniye Vedomosti* published by the Church authorities, lived in fear of thieves and carefully shuttered the windows of its small cottages every night. . . .

And yet the police were filled with apprehension that Maxim Gorky's appearance in this town might arouse untoward disturbances. The Superintendent of the Arzamas police received the following confidential notification:

"In the near future Alexei Maximovich Peshkov (M. Gorky), who is under the surveillance of the police, will be arriving in Arzamas to take up his abode there.

"Immediately on his arrival in Arzamas you are instructed to place him under surveillance and take all necessary precautions that there are no disturbances when Peshkov is met."

Gorky moved into a roomy wooden house. A garden was attached to the house in which an old linden tree grew.

Spring had only just drawn to a close and, after the Crimea with its seemingly metallic foliage, every tree in Arzamas was a source of delight to Gorky.

He went for long walks in the woods and to a spot known as Moist Hollow.

"Now this one tree alone," he would say patting a small silver fir affectionately, "is better than any Crimean landscape."

He took delight also in the green fields which stretched beyond the town and the river Tesha which teemed with perch and pike.

The police kept the house under strict surveillance. This is what Gorky wrote in a letter to Chekhov:

"It is quiet here and restful and the air is delicious. There are gardens everywhere, nightingales sing in the gardens and police spies lie hidden under the bushes. There are nightingales in every garden but police spies only in mine, I think. They sit under my windows in the darkness of night and try to get a glimpse of how I spread sedition through Russia. And not seeing how it is done they grunt disconsolately and scare the inmates of my house."

Everything that Gorky did was regarded with profound suspicion by the police. If he gave a silver coin to a beggar a policeman would be bound to snatch it from the man and try it between his teeth so as to make sure that the suspect Peshkov was not circulating counterfeit money.

Sometimes Gorky would beckon to one of the police spies sitting under the window and then a conversation on the following lines would take place:

"You're a spy, aren't you?"

"No!"

"You're lying. Aren't you a spy?"

"I'm not, so help me God!"

"Have you been long at the job?"

"No, only recently...."

Once in a while such an important Arzamas personage as Superintendent Danilov would pass by Gorky's house. A big, corpulent man, with a large pipe between his teeth, he would cast a searching look through the window as he rode past on his horse. Evidently he was firmly convinced that if Gorky was plotting a revolution in Russia then he, Superintendent Danilov, would be bound to notice it at once and nip it in the bud.

Superintendent Danilov, however, was sadly mistaken. In spite of the plain-clothes men under the windows and the police spies in the bushes Gorky continued to participate in the revolutionary struggle during his stay in Arzamas.

The population of Arzamas did not consist of priests, merchants and petty officials alone. Other people also lived there—workers from the small tanneries, shoemakers and saddlers. It was of these saddlers and shoemakers that Lenin wrote in one of his books that they work for their masters for fourteen hours a day and receive a mere pittance in return.

"That is why," observed Lenin, "the saddlers are pale, emaciated and dying off."

It was these "pale, emaciated" working-men that came to Gorky, slipping through the cordon of police and spies.

While he was living in Arzamas Gorky took part in a daring revolutionary enterprise.

The Ponetayev Monastery near Arzamas was known as a hot-bed of counter-revolution. Adjoining the monastery was a licensed wineshop. The Nizhni-Novgorod revolutionaries decided together with Gorky to "take over" the shop. After all, who would ever dream of looking for revolutionaries in a licensed wineshop in such a hole-and-corner place, and next door to a monastery at that?

The plan was a success: a carpenter by the name of Lebedev, an active Nizhni-Novgorod revolutionary, was put in charge of the shop. The ex-carpenter sold vodka to the monks and the pilgrims who flocked to the monastery on religious holidays, while in the backroom of the shop the revolutionaries set up a secret printing press. The leaflets and proclamations printed here were distributed all over the province.

A long time passed before the authorities paid any attention to the wineshop at Ponetayevka and, when they did, it was only by pure chance. Thieves broke into the shop. News of the burglary reached the ears of the police. At any moment they could be expected to appear at the scene of the robbery. Fortunately, however, by the time the police did arrive to investigate the case, the printing press and the shopkeeper had already disappeared without leaving a trace.

The printing press was saved. The secret of the Ponetayevka wineshop was never disclosed.

Superintendent Danilov received regular reports that a light would be showing in the window of Gorky's study all night long. This was hardly to the Superintendent's liking:

"Our suspect does not sleep enough, he works very late."

Gorky wrote a lot, engrossed in his work.

He was busy on a play concerning which he stated in a letter to Chekhov that not to like it would be impossible, and for him not to work on it would be criminal.

Chapter XI
ON THE STAGE OF THE ART THEATRE

In the old Moscow theatres, in the Maly Theatre or the Korsh, the heavy curtains of red plush embroidered with gold would rise to the din of an orchestra just as in an opera-house. The actors would rant and stamp their feet and preferred parts which gave them an opportunity of shooting with a revolver. In the auditorium of the theatre silk skirts would rustle, spurs ring, people would converse in a loud tone and clap or hiss as the case might be.

In the new theatre they knew how to value silence. The modest curtain did not rise, but opened slowly like the pages of a book.

The people on the stage tried to keep a lock on their feelings and to gesticulate less. Sometimes they preferred to be silent and together with the audience to listen to the soft patter of the raindrops, the early morning song of the birds, the clatter of a departing carriage or the ticking of a clock.

No encores were given and the audience did not applaud.

The performers in this theatre were young actors or amateurs. One of the ablest actors was a teacher of calligraphy.

It was people with a deep feeling for the new art that created the Art Theatre.

Gorky paid a visit to the Art Theatre during one of his trips to Moscow. Chekhov's play *Uncle Vanya* was running.

Gorky saw Uncle Vanya sitting over his accounts, saw Waffle quietly strumming the strings of a guitar, saw Dr. Astrov looking at the map of Africa which for some reason or other hung in the room, saw how Professor Serebryakov did not want anybody to play the piano—watched everyday human life being unravelled before his eyes and, as he himself admitted, "cried like an old woman."

Gorky returned home from the theatre which so treasured silence as if he were stunned.

He wrote to Chekhov and this letter was one of the most fervid that ever came from Gorky's pen:

"You can't say outright and clearly what this play arouses in your soul but, looking at the heroes, I felt as though a blunt saw were rending me in two. The teeth kept passing to and fro across my heart, and my heart shrank under them, groaning, torn asunder. As far as I was concerned it was a frightful experience. Yes, *Uncle Vanya* is something entirely new in dramatic art.

"In the last act, when the doctor after a long pause speaks of how hot it is in Africa, I trembled with admiration at your talent, and fear for people, for our bleak, poverty-stricken life."

Gorky regretted that he lived in Nizhni-Novgorod, where he was deprived of the possibility of visiting this wonderful theatre.

Then they met in the Crimea—Gorky and the Art Theatre. They had come to Yalta, on a visit to the man who had written *Uncle Vanya*—to Chekhov.

It was springtime. The flowers planted by the author in the garden of his white summer house were in bloom. . . .

Chekhov and Gorky strolled along the cobbled streets of Yalta, along the white embankment and in the evening they would go to the gloomy little theatre, where the members of the Art Theatre staged the plays of their favourite playwright.

Chekhov exhorted Gorky to write a play. The Art Theatre also expected him to.

And now, in Arzamas, Gorky set to work in what was for him an entirely new field. He wrote his first play—*Philistines*—portraying the bitter life of the Bessemenov family.

Gorky worked hard on the play, which did not come easily to him. The dramatic form was unfamiliar to him. He wrote and re-wrote it, recalling the jocular advice of a certain man of letters: Write a five-act tragedy and after a year recast it as a three-act drama. Put it away for another year and then re-write it as a one-act vaudeville and then, after the lapse of yet another year, throw the vaudeville into the fire. . . .

Gorky did not throw *Philistines* into the fire. Nevertheless he was dissatisfied with it. It seemed to him that the play was too scrappy and flat.

"I don't like it," Gorky admitted in a letter to Chekhov. "I'll do another in the winter. I've set my mind on it. And if that doesn't come out properly—I'll write a dozen more but I'll get what I want! It must be compact and beautiful like a piece of music."

It was precisely this music that sounded in Chekhov's plays on the stage of the Art Theatre—the music of simple human language. And recalling this Gorky set to work on a new play.

In *Philistines* he had portrayed people whom he had known from childhood, people who lived in small urban houses, in the stuffy atmosphere of pots and pans and samovars and icons and hoarded belongings stuffed away in chests.

In his new play Gorky turned to the *bosyaks* for his

material, to the slum dwellers of Millionaire Street in Nizhni-Novgorod and the "Crystal Palace" in Kazan.

While still in the Crimea, sitting one evening on the porch in the gathering dusk, Gorky had mused aloud about his new play: the hero is a former butler to a wealthy family whom the vicissitudes of life have brought to a doss house, from which he has never been able to extricate himself. The man's most treasured possession is the collar of a dress shirt—the one object that links him with his former life. The doss house is crowded, everybody there hates everyone else. But in the last act spring comes, the stage is flooded with sunlight and the inmates of the doss house leave their squalid dwelling and forget the hatred they bear for each other....

This was how Gorky sketched in rough outline the play which he subsequently first entitled *The Lower Depths of Life*.

Gorky had rubbed shoulders with the heroes of his play in the market places, on the highroads and wharves, had huddled together with them in the same bunks and sat round campfires with them at night.... The figure of Satin, for instance, he sketched on the lines of an ex-Post Office master he had once known who had served a term in prison. The man had roamed about the streets of Nizhni-Novgorod with his chest bared, begging alms in French from the womenfolk he met on the way. There was something picturesque, romantic about him and the women would be moved to give him a copper....

When the *Lower Depths* was finished a pre-reading of the play was arranged in the Art Theatre.

Gorky read the play himself.

When he came to the scene in which Luka murmurs words of comfort and solace to the dying Anna the actors listened intently, with bated breath. His voice trembled and broke. He stopped reading and silently dashed a tear away with his hand. He tried to go on but after a word or two he had to stop again and openly burst into tears. . . .

The government only very reluctantly permitted Gorky's plays to be staged. The censors ruthlessly blue-pencilled his manuscripts. In *Philistines* they picked on the phrase "the merchant Romanoff's wife" which seemed particularly suspicious to them, taking it for an allusion to the Royal Family. The censors insisted on Romanoff being changed to Ivanov. . . .

On the day of the dress rehearsal of *Philistines* the theatre was cordoned off by a posse of police and mounted gendarmes. One might have thought that it was not a dress rehearsal that was about to be staged but a battle royal. On the first night of *Philistines* and for several nights after that the authorities gave orders for the ushers to be replaced by police officers. The government was apprehensive that the students might invade the theatre and organize a demonstration in Gorky's honour. . . .

"When a man is tired of lying on one side he turns over on the other, but when he is tired of the conditions in which he lives he only grumbles. Then make an effort—and turn over!"

These words were spoken from the stage by one of the heroes of the play, the young railwayman Nil.

And the audience responded to them with a storm of applause.

Gorky's second play—*Lower Depths*—was accorded an even more rousing reception.

"Lies—there you have the religion of slaves and task-masters." These words of Satin the censor prohibited from being spoken on the stage. But he did not succeed in obliterating the underlying sense of the play. Every one of its lines breathed fiery protest against a system of society under which the bulk of the people were deprived of their right to live.

A system which permitted people to be degraded to the

level of "creatures that once were men," into denizens of Kostilyev's doss house—is based on a lie, and this lie must be torn up by the roots. That was how the gallery, the students, understood the play.

The first night of *Lower Depths* turned into a mighty demonstration in Gorky's honour. Time and again the audience called for the author. With a look of bewilderment on his face Gorky came out on to the stage, forgetting in his embarrassment to take the cigarette out of his mouth. . . .

But this demonstration in his honour was more than a mere theatrical success.

Chapter XII

THREE REVOLUTIONS

January 9th

> "You must shoot, General, always shoot!"
> (*Nicholas II in a conversation with General Kazbek, the Commandant of Vladivostok*).

The storm predicted in the *Song of the Stormy Petrel* finally broke. Came the year 1905, a year in which blood flowed freely in the square facing the gloomy palace of the Tsar, on the hills of distant Manchuria, in the courtyards of police stations and snowbound way-stations, in the back streets of Moscow and on the blue decks of warships.

Revolutionary events flared up from the very first days of the year. On January 9th the priest Gapon, a secret agent of the *Okhranka* who harboured dreams of a grand career, headed a monster demonstration of St. Petersburg workers to the Winter Palace. The workers carried a petition to the Tsar. In it they wrote:

"We, the working men of St. Petersburg, our wives, our children and our helpless old parents, have come to Thee, our Sovereign, to seek truth and protection....

"We can bear it no longer, Oh Sire. Our patience is exhausted. The dreaded moment has arrived when we would rather die than bear these intolerable sufferings any longer...."

Two hundred thousand men and women marched to see the Tsar—a desperate, deluded mass of humanity. A ray of hope still flickered in their breasts that in the Winter Palace they would find someone who would protect them from their oppressors.

The government knew beforehand of the forthcoming demonstration, as also did the Tsar. Orders were issued to the troops to be in fighting readiness. A kinsman of the Tsar, the Grand Duke Vladimir, declared at Court that only the blood of the people could save the dynasty. It was he who was placed in command of the troops.

On that day Gorky was in the streets together with the workers. He heard the sinister bugle call giving the signal to open fire.

It was a day of horror, a horror that "seared like a red hot iron."

But it was not only horror that gripped the crowd. Gorky heard the people fling in the faces of their murderers:

"You thought you were killing the people, were you?"
"The people can't be killed! We'll show you yet...."
"It's the Tsar you killed, understand?"

On the morning of January 9th the workers still believed that they could find protection in the Tsar, and they went to him with a petition in their hands. By noon of the same day they were looking for arms and, not finding any, they made shift with bricks and cobblestones. Gapon had vanished; the petitioners of the Tsar had become fighters against the Tsar, and January 9th was the first day of the first Russian revolution.

Gorky returned home shaken to the marrow and immediately wrote an appeal "To All Russian Citizens and to Public Opinion of the Countries of Europe."

He denounced what had taken place on the streets of St. Petersburg as premeditated, deliberate murder and boldly impeached the hangman-in-chief—the Tsar.

Gorky called for an open struggle to overthrow the autocracy.

The original of the appeal fell into the hands of the police. The *Okhranka* knew the revolutionary writer's handwriting well. Two days after the January 9th events Gorky was arrested. He was taken to the Fortress of Peter and Paul—the prison in which only those charged with high treason were confined.

After incessant requests Gorky was finally permitted the "wherewithals for literary occupation." Here, in his cell, he started work on *Children of the Sun*, a play over which fell the sinister shadow of January 9th. One of the characters in the play says:

"Whenever I hear anything harsh or bitter, whenever I see anything red, a gnawing horror fills my soul again and before my eyes rises a vision of that brutal mob, blood-stained faces and pools of warm, red blood in the sand. . . ."

Gorky, however, did not lose heart. He introduced many humorous touches into the play and as he did so he could not refrain from laughing. The warders were so astounded at hearing the prisoner laugh that they called out the governor of the prison. . . .

When several years before Gorky had been confined in the Nizhni-Novgorod prison a wave of protest had swept over the whole of Russia. Now the whole of Europe came out in the writer's defence.

"Gorky does not belong to Russia alone but to the whole world," Anatole France declared at a meeting in Paris.

Protests poured into St. Petersburg from Germany, Portugal, Italy and Belgium. The demand for Gorky's release was supported by the physicist Pierre Curie and the sculptor Auguste Rodin, by the socialist leader Jean Jaurès and the landscape painter Claude Monet— men famous throughout Europe, and all friends of the writer whom the tsarist authorities stupidly persisted in calling an "artisan of the city of Nizhni-Novgorod."

"Your arrest has brought a veritable hornet's nest about our ears in Europe," an officer of the gendarmes told Gorky when he was being interrogated in the fortress. Seven years before this very same officer had questioned Gorky in Metekh Castle....

And again, for the third time, the tsarist government was forced to yield. Gorky was released from prison.

It is more than probable that he would not have lived much longer had he been detained in this prison where the very stones seemed to devour people. After a month's confinement he had begun to spit blood.

Bloody Sunday, as January 9th came to be known amongst the people, was never forgotten. The workers began to make preparations for an armed struggle, for an insurrection. The uprising took place at the end of the year.

The Moscow workers came out on strike. Events immediately took on a serious turn. The crowds which only recently had scattered at the mere cry of "The Cossacks are coming!" now attacked the Cossacks themselves.

The revolution of 1905 was coming to a head.

Gorky was living in Moscow at the time, collecting funds for the purchase of arms. His flat opposite the Riding School resembled a regular military camp. Here rifles, revolvers and hand grenades were stored, and here they were distributed to members of the fighting squads. The "law-abiding" citizens who lived in the same house listened horror-stricken to the crack of rifle-shots coming from Gorky's apartment: the Caucasian students who acted as the writer's bodyguard had set up a rifle range in his rooms.

Gorky saw the workers building barricades, he saw detachments of regulars rake the streets with rifle fire and cannons pounding the Krasnaya Presnya district.

The Moscow uprising was crushed but the revolution was not suppressed.

Typewritten copies of a letter from Gorky to the workers were disseminated all over Russia. In this letter he stated:

"The proletariat has not been vanquished, although it has suffered losses. The revolution has been strengthened by new hopes while its forces have grown to a colossal extent. . . .

"The Russian proletariat is marching forward to a decisive victory, for it is the only class which is morally strong and conscientious, and has faith in its destiny in Russia. What I say is true and this truth will be confirmed by all honest and unbiassed historians."

It was in 1905, on the eve of the Moscow uprising that Gorky met Lenin for the first time.

The truth with which Gorky addressed himself to the Russian people was the same truth as Lenin spoke about the revolution.

And history corroborated this truth far quicker than the most honest historian could have assumed.

* * *

Friends warned Gorky that a warrant had been issued for his arrest. He left for abroad, to Germany and France and then to America.

In New York Gorky continued to denounce the tsarist government. He addressed public meetings and published articles in the press, appealing among other things to world public opinion to prevent the foreign bankers from granting a loan to the Tsar the purpose of which was to suppress the revolutionary movement in Russia.

It was while he was living in America, in a log cabin hidden away in a garden in the Adirondacks, that Gorky set to work on his novel *Mother*.

Gorky chose his heroes for this novel from amongst the Sormovo workers. Pavel Vlassov and his mother,

Nilovna, were drawn from actual life, from people whom he knew well, as, for instance, Pyotr Zalomov—a revolutionary worker who had been sentenced to prison for taking part in a May Day demonstration of the Sormovo workers—and his mother, who was also active in the revolutionary movement. In the guise of a nun Pyotr's mother had disseminated revolutionary literature all over the Nizhni-Novgorod region.

This splendid woman was no exception. Gorky knew the mother of the Kadomtsevs, a family of revolutionaries, who had been tried in Ufa for helping her son to escape from prison by smuggling bombs to him with which he had made a breach in the prison wall. Gorky could mention the names of scores of other mothers who had been tried together with their children.

Some of these heroic women Gorky knew personally. The tsarist government realized the enormous revolutionary significance of this novel. The magazine in which Part One of *Mother* was published was confiscated, while Part Two was so mutilated by the censor that it was hardly recognizable. Entire chapters were deleted.

The government instituted legal proceedings against Gorky. An announcement appeared in the *Vedomosti* of the St. Petersburg Municipality that "Alexei Maximovich Peshkov, an artisan belonging to the Nizhni-Novgorod paper hangers' guild, was wanted by the police on a warrant issued by the St. Petersburg district court." But Gorky, fortunately, was out of their reach.

After his revolutionary activities abroad Gorky could no longer think of returning to Russia and so he settled down in Italy, on the Island of Capri.

It was during this period of his life that he became very friendly with Lenin. This happened in 1907, at the Fifth Congress of the Russian Social-Democratic Party in London, to which Gorky had been invited by the Bolshevik leader.

Every day an ancient four-wheeler, resembling the contraptions in which Dickens' heroes had travelled, took Gorky to one of the suburbs of London, to the wooden church with lancet windows in which the Congress was being held. It had been impossible to hire more suitable premises.

Leaning against one of the pillars Gorky would watch the congress delegates for hours on end and listen to the passionate debates between the Mensheviks and the Bolsheviks.

". . . At last Vladimir Ilyich walked up to the rostrum with his brisk stride, pronouncing the word 'Comrades' in his guttural way. It seemed to me at first that he spoke badly but almost a minute later I, like everybody else, was held spellbound by his speech. This was the first time I had ever heard anybody speak so simply on such intricate questions of policy. Here was an orator who made no attempt to coin beautiful phrases but was clear as clear could be, laying bare with a wonderful ease the exact meaning of his words."

This was how Gorky recalled his first impression of Lenin as a speaker.

From that time on an intimate friendship began between Gorky and Lenin.

Vladimir Ilyich visited Gorky at Capri. Here, resting from his intense labours, Lenin played chess, went fishing, explored the rocky tracks and admired the golden play of colours on the gorse-covered heaths. . . . Of an evening Gorky would recall his wanderings over Russia while Lenin listened eagerly to his enthralling narratives.

The Capri fishermen became very fond of Gorky's guest. After Lenin had left they often asked Gorky:

"The Tsar won't catch him, will he?"

In his letters to Gorky Lenin always expressed a deep and friendly concern and a lively interest in his work and health.

Lenin called Gorky the foremost representative of proletarian art.

"There is no doubt," Lenin wrote, "that Gorky is an outstanding literary genius who has done much and will do still more on behalf of the world proletarian movement."

When the tsarist government proclaimed an amnesty in 1913 Lenin advised Gorky to return to Russia.

Gorky left Capri and settled down in St. Petersburg. A year later the World War broke out.

The author of these lines had occasion to meet Gorky about this time at a meeting of one of the revolutionary students' circles. Gorky was speaking on the subject of the war, telling how two soldiers at the front, a Russian and a German, had simultaneously plunged their bayonets into each other and had remained standing locked in mortal embrace. . . .

These two soldiers embodied, as it were, the destiny of the peoples doomed to a senseless and ignominious mutual extermination.

Gorky's face clouded with sorrow when he spoke about the men at the front. But his sorrow changed to wrath when he declaimed against the people in the rear—against the petty shopkeepers who were ready to exalt the most despicable crime into a national virtue.

In one of his public speeches Gorky said:

"We are witnessing the mad revels of some monstrous hog which is attempting to root up the whole world with its snout."

The *Letopis* (*Annals*) published by Gorky took its stand against the imperialist war. It was in the columns of this magazine that Mayakovsky's poem "War and Peace" first appeared.

Mayakovsky was little known at the time. The public saw in him only a literary scandalmonger in a yellow jacket and silk top hat. But he was no scandalmonger, he was a rebel and in "War and Peace" he, to use his own expression, "spat his rhymes in the war's face."

The winter of the third year of the war seemed to drag on interminably. In the editorial office of *Letopis* the main topic of conversation was the disturbances at the factories and plants.

At one of the meetings of the editorial board Gorky said:

"We are nearing the denouement."

A week later the blue train of the Tsar was held up at Dno while on its way from Petrograd to General Staff Headquarters and Nicholas II affixed his signature to his abdication. This was in February 1917.

* * *

"I have a vivid recollection," recalls V. Desnitsky, one of Gorky's friends, "of one of the first meetings between Gorky and Lenin after the 1917 events.

"This was shortly after the Socialist-Revolutionary Kaplan had made her attempt on Lenin's life. Vladimir Ilyich was in high spirits and, rubbing his hands as he smiled at Gorky, kept on urging him:

"'Come on, man, out with it! Let's hear what's troubling you. . . .'

"Yakov Sverdlov also dropped in to see the two friends. Vladimir Ilyich was describing the attempt on his life; he spoke calmly about it and of how the operation had passed, giving a detailed account of the case history of his sickness.

"'*A la guerre, comme à la guerre*! And it won't be over so soon either. . . .'

"He pressed us to eat.

"'Try some of this cheese. The bread is really fresh and soft. Help yourself to the cherries, we only just bought them. . . .'

"The meal was very frugal indeed. The host was not even aware of the fact that he had no tea in the house and so I slipped down to the office and asked one of the staff, an old friend of mine from Nizhni-Novgorod, for a spoonful of tea for the Chairman of the Council of People's Commissars.

"There was an anxious look on Gorky's face when he questioned Vladimir Ilyich about his health and whether the wound would have any effect on his ability to work. Vladimir Ilyich carefully but seemingly without any effort raised his arm, stretched it out, bent it and then stretched it out again. Gorky ran his finger over Lenin's collar bone and the muscles of his arm. Vladimir Ilyich stood stockstill the whole while, looking searchingly at him. Gorky's fingers seemed to speak of more than the mere wish to reassure himself of his friend's physical fitness. The impression one got was that Gorky wanted to convince himself again and again that it was precisely Lenin in whom the strength and the will of millions were concentrated and that from Lenin emanated the bright light that illuminated the path into the future. . . .

"And he did convince himself."

And Lenin, for his part, never ceased to take a solicitous interest in Gorky. When Gorky's health took a turn for the worse in 1921 Lenin insisted that he go abroad for treatment.

Gorky again went to Italy, this time settling down in Sorrento.

From there he closely followed everything that was going on in the Land of Soviets, multiplying and strengthening the ties that bound him to the country of his birth.

And when in 1928, the year of his sixtieth birthday, Gorky returned to the U.S.S.R. the whole country welcomed him as its great writer and revolutionary.

In 1932 the Soviet Union celebrated the fortieth anniversary of Gorky's literary activities.

"The name of Maxim Gorky," the Central Committee of the C.P.S.U.(B.) stated in its message of greetings, "is near and dear to the working people of the Land of Soviets and far beyond its borders as the name of a great writer and revolutionary, as the name of a fighter against tsarism."

Gorky's jubilee developed into a nationwide celebration.

Gorky's close friendship with Lenin directed his impetuous spirit into revolutionary channels. His close friendship with Stalin determined his work and his labours during the latter years of his life.

After his return to the U.S.S.R. Gorky took his place at the helm of the literary life of the Soviet Union. He founded and edited several magazines, initiated the publication of *The History of Factories and Plants* and *The History of the Civil War* and guided the activities of the Soviet Writers' Union.

The vast scope of Gorky's activities claimed an enormous amount of his time and energy, but he never for a moment ceased his literary work. He wrote a sequel to *Clim Samghin*, a series of articles and several plays including *Yegor Bulichoff*, which is admitted to be one of the most significant and brilliant of all Gorky's productions.

"I must write four more books," Gorky told his friends in the last year of his life. "I absolutely must. Four books at the rate of one every two years. Eight years." And old as he was, Gorky could have achieved much more, could have created many new heroes, could have written many more books.

But in June 1936 he suddenly fell ill. His sickness from the very outset took an extremely grave turn. He paid little heed to his heavy breathing or his uneven pulse, so engrossed was he with what had constituted the essence of his life all these years—the thought of his work and his country. He could only breathe and speak with difficulty but, in the intervals between taking oxygen, he discussed the new Constitution of the Soviet

Union and asked to be shown the newspaper in which the text of the Constitution was published. He spoke feelingly of Stalin, often recalled Lenin and his first meeting with him. . . .

Even when he was delirious he never once complained or uttered a single word about himself.

He was conscious of the fact that he was dying.

On the evening of June 18th he lost consciousness. The snatches of words that passed his lips while he was in this state showed what he was thinking of during his last hours:

"War is impending. . . . We must be prepared. . . . We mustn't be caught unawares. . . ."

He died early the next morning. It subsequently transpired that his death had been deliberately contrived by the enemies of the Soviet people, by the Trotskyite-Bukharinite scoundrels who had been in the pay of the German fascist Intelligence Service. It was they who brought about his death, realizing that the tremendous influence he exerted on public opinion hindered them from carrying out their infamous designs.

The news of Gorky's death spread like wildfire through the country. The sentiments of the millions who mourned Gorky were expressed by V. M. Molotov in his speech at the memorial meeting held in the Red Square:

"In parting today with Alexei Maximovich Gorky we, his friends, and countless readers and admirers of his works, feel as though a glorious page in our lives has been turned over for all time. . . .

"After Lenin the death of Gorky is the heaviest loss our country and humanity has suffered."

Chapter XIII
WRITER AND FIGHTER

The fate of many Russian writers who came from the ranks of the people, from the ranks of the commoners, was tragic indeed. Gorky recalls this in one of his articles. Pomyalovski was flogged four hundred times in all during his term of tuition in the seminary. Levitov was publicly thrashed before his class, and as he himself expressed it: "They thrashed the soul out of my body." When Reshetnikov was a lad of fourteen he was haled before a court and sentenced to two years imprisonment. These writers who enriched Russian literature with such outstanding works as the *Essays of a Seminarist*, *Philistine Happiness* and *Podlipovtsi* knew only too well what poverty and obscurity meant.

Hardly had they reached manhood than they died in some squalid hovel or infirmary bed.

They left behind them only their manuscripts and these manuscripts resembled at times the disjointed reasonings of a suicide—so permeated were they with melancholy and despair.

Gorky's life was still harder. It was a synthesis, as it were, of all the trials that had fallen to the lot of his predecessors. He had been flogged like Pomyalovski and publicly thrashed like Levitov. He had worked as a longshoreman on the Volga just as Kuschevski had on the Neva. True, Gorky was already a grown man when he was sent to prison for the first time, but at sixteen he had been one of the "gaolbirds" in Semyonov's bakery, an experience which in all probability was far worse than any prison.

At four Gorky had contracted cholera, at eight—smallpox. While working as an errand-boy in the shoestore he had scalded himself terribly with some hot soup. He had been flogged both at home and by the masters he worked for, and on one occasion had actually been taken to hospital, where the doctor who treated him extracted forty-two splinters from his body. That was after he had been whipped with pine rods. A hunter in the woods had fired a full charge of shot into him. He had been almost murdered by the mob in the Ukrainian village of Kandibovka and had barely escaped with his life from the kulaks who had assaulted him in Krasnovydovo, a village on the Volga. And once, while working on a barge, he had seriously injured himself by falling into the hold.

Fatal illnesses, brutal people and bad luck—this was what made up the biography of Gorky in his younger days.

He was at an early age when life began to buffet him about and he realized the horror of the existence of the men and women who surrounded him.

One of his favourite pastimes as a youngster was to make his way in the company of his friends to a hollow. There the children would make themselves comfortable on a large log at the bottom, and sing. Gorky acted as choir master. He always chose sad songs. A crowd would gather on the edge of the hollow and stand there for a long time listening to the children singing. Their sad songs appealed to them.

And this was the lad who, after traversing an infinitely difficult and painful path, later on became a great writer and brought to literature not only the grim truth of how the down-trodden Russian men and women lived in the lower depths but also a spirited call to a better life.

What was the source of Gorky's irrepressible optimism?

Much of it he inherited from his father, from the cabinet maker and paper hanger Maxim Savvatievich. It was fostered in him as a boy by Akulina Ivanovna, his splendid old grandmother. And later on, when Alosha Peshkov became one of the denizens of the Nizhni-Novgorod garrets and basements, he absorbed it from books.

But could this belief in life last for long?

One of Gorky's heroines, Old Izergill, says:

"When a man is bent on doing something big he's always bound to come up to the mark and show his mettle whenever it's humanly possible. In life, you know, there's always room for heroic deeds."

Gorky's heroic deed was the life he lived. He went out to meet it half way as though he were eager to learn in advance all the trials and tribulations in store for him—Alexei Peshkov, the penniless tramp and man of odd jobs.

And as though sensing that the people he chanced across on the long and intricate maze of roads he travelled would one day become the heroes of his stories, novels and dramas, he not only observed them but ferreted them out and dogged their steps like an untiring hunter.

Once during his wanderings Gorky came to a small country town as dull as a tedious dream. But in the shabby hotel there he caught sight of a man in a shantung jacket who roused his curiosity. Gorky forgot all about the dull little town, about the road that still lay ahead of him and followed the man through street after street, to a restaurant and then to a churchyard until he finally convinced himself that the man he was interested in was a mere well-fed philistine, as dull as the town itself.

Disappointments of this kind happened often enough, but after each experience he would accrue a grain of new knowledge and store it away in his mind.

He brought to literature not only a thorough knowledge of the people whom the old writers had never dreamed of selecting for their heroes, but also a knowledge of the country, of peoples who had been completely overlooked by men of letters, rivers and songs and highways.

In one story he remarks through the lips of his hero:

"Speaking about Russia, brother, you just can't rate things off hand. Every region has its own soul."

Gorky has left us descriptions of Wild Heaths in Moldavia and the forests of Kerzhents, the Ukrainian highways and the Kuban *stanitsas*. And through all the scenes and landscapes which Gorky unfolds before us, he once tramped himself stick in hand with a knapsack on his back.

Not all at once did Gorky learn to make full use of his knowledge.

Fame came to him quite early, but his road to his art was nevertheless long.

He began to keep a diary ever since he was almost ten years of age and this was his first book, a book which he wrote for only one reader—for himself.

Later on, when a young lad in Kazan, he dabbled in verse. His poems were poor and even after he decided to try his hand at prose he continued to write in semi-rhythmic, singsong phrases.

"In general," Gorky recalled, "I tried to write 'beautifully'. . . ."

"'The sea laughed,' I wrote and for a long time I sincerely thought it good. In search for a beautiful phrase I would be always sinning against exactness, put things in the wrong places, or people in the wrong light."

Two writers whose opinions Gorky valued very highly, namely Tolstoy and Chekhov, pointed this out to the young writer.

"Your oven is not where it should be," Tolstoy said to Gorky after reading his *Twenty-Six Men and a Girl*. It turned out that the flames from the oven could not possibly light up the workers in the way Gorky had described it.

And Chekhov remarked about one of Gorky's heroines: "You've given her three ears, old man—she has one on her chin. Just look!"

These were mere details, of course, explained by the fact that he lacked the skill as yet to write lucidly and simply and to pick and choose his words. He realized more and more how difficult and how necessary this absolute precision and simplicity was for an artist.

Chekhov remarked about *Malva*—one of Gorky's early stories.

"You just read: 'The sea laughed' and you stopped short. Do you really think you paused there because it's good, picturesque? Of course not! You stopped short simply because you could not grasp the idea at once yourself: how's that—the sea—and suddenly laughing? The sea doesn't laugh or cry. It murmurs, splashes, sparkles.... Take a look at Tolstoy: the sun rises, birds sing.... Nobody weeps and nobody laughs. And yet that is the most important thing—simplicity...."

This art, the extremely difficult art of writing simply, Gorky studied long and assiduously. He learned much from other writers and he learned much from the people—that great creator of the language. He read and re-read the classics, his favourite authors, with the utmost care—Tolstoy, Flaubert, Chekhov, Dickens and Leskov, but at the same time he listened intently to the rough and ready speech of the people amongst whom he lived: workmen, tradespeople, soldiers, bargehaulers, actors, bakers, choirboys and sailors....

And finally he attained that high level of art when beauty and simplicity and truth are indivisible, when beauty *is* simplicity and truth.

He learned to draw pen pictures of faces, rivers, houses, the sky, the woods, in words so exact that they engrave themselves on the reader's mind as though carved out of precious stones.

Here is a scene painted by Gorky in his later years:

"We were sitting in the garden, in the shade of the cherry trees which were richly adorned with beads of amethyst fruit. It was evening, and the stifling heat foreboded a storm. Filmy-grey tufts of clouds frothed the sky, which was the colour of skimmed milk; shadows flitted across the garden and it was strange to see the leaves hanging so motionlessly."

With the keen and observant eye of a great writer Gorky learned to distinguish the finest shades of colour about him and to store them in the pigeon-holes of his memory.

Even in his childhood Gorky astonished everybody with his splendid memory. His Grandfather used to say that he had "the memory of an elephant." Once Gorky saw a map of Australia in the hands of one of his friends, a high-school boy by the name of Yevreinov. Gorky took the map and examined it. The next day he knew all the islands, rivers, mountains and cities marked on the map by heart.

When Gorky became a writer his wonderful memory resurrected a map not of Australia but of Russia—of life on the banks of the Volga, in the mountain districts of the Crimea and Caucasus and innumerable towns and cities throughout the country.

This was a map of cruel injustice and untold human suffering.

When the Art Theatre was preparing the settings for *Lower Depths* the stage director and the decorator required a photograph of a doss house. Gorky had to explain to them that the only way to get one was to take a flashlight photo since daylight never penetrated into the doss houses.

Gorky was the first to tell of the lives of people whose black and dreary existences could not be recorded on a negative in the ordinary way.

But although the mole-like lives led by Gorky's *bosyaks* was frightful indeed, still more frightful were those of Gorky's philistines.

When Gorky passed his examinations in the third class at school he was awarded a Bible, a copy of Krylov's fables and a certificate.

Gorky sold the books at a bookstall for fifty kopecks—his grandmother was sick at the time and penniless.

On the certificate he wrote:

"Our pigsty of a Kunavino." *

Gorky was ten years old at the time but he had already seen for himself what a piggish life the smug denizens of Kunavino were living.

Many of Gorky's stories, novels and plays can be classified under this general heading—"Our pigsty of a Kunavino," for life was foul not only in Kunavino.

But Gorky did not merely record the sad and dark sides of Russian life.

Even when he was still a youngster and rather hazy on questions of spelling he already had a firm opinion on the purpose and aims of literature.

Once in Kazan he happened to attend a lecture on Shakespeare. The lecturer in a rich and musical voice, declared:

"The one purpose of literature is to appease the soul."

But Peshkov, the baker, did not agree with him. He jotted down the phrase in his diary together with the comment: "It's a damn lie!"

---

* Kunavino — a suburb of Nizhni-Novgorod which was inhabited by the lower middle class and the poor.—*Ed.*

He knew that literature had a much loftier purpose, and that this purpose was not to appease but to rouse a man's soul.

And subsequently, when he became a writer, he said through the lips of one of his heroes:

"People ought to have hedgehogs stuck under their scalps, so that they should never rest content."

And Gorky's words stung, roused, and burrowed just like a hedgehog ever deeper into his readers' conscience.

In those pre-revolutionary years, when Gorky was still a newcomer to literature and lived in Nizhni-Novgorod, a tall man in a long overcoat of English cut and a flaming red cap which aroused the admiration of all the street urchins in the neighbourhood would be a constant visitor to his house. The police spies who kept Gorky's house under observation knew as soon as they saw the man that before long a crowd of people would gather in the street in front of the house to hear the famous Chaliapin sing.

Gorky had become friendly with Chaliapin while still in Kazan. The two men, the baker Peshkov and the cobbler Chaliapin, had applied one day at a local theatre to try for a job in the choir. Gorky was taken on, while Chaliapin was rejected as having no voice.

The former baker and the former cobbler both achieved world fame, but their roads parted.

In 1902, at a celebration in Chaliapin's honour, Gorky declared bluntly in a speech that cut like a lash:

"You are a genius, but your songs are being wasted in the gilded salons of the wives of the Zamoskvorechye merchants. Inspire the souls of the unfortunate and oppressed. Then only will you be truly great."

Chaliapin did not follow this advice and, when the revolution burst into the "gilded salons," he left the country and betrayed the people from whose ranks he had sprung.

Gorky addressed his songs to the people. And when

the people accomplished the greatest revolution in world history and set about the task of creating a new social order, Gorky gave them not only his songs but also all the energy of a fighter, the initiative of a builder and the learning of one of the most educated men of our times.

Gorky's biography during the last ten years of his life is the biography not merely of a writer but of an outstanding Soviet public figure, the acknowledged leader of the literary life of the U.S.S.R., a fighter for culture, a revolutionary who stood shoulder to shoulder with the finest men in the world, men who with their creative genius were serving the cause of the emancipation of humanity.

The life and struggle of great men is directed towards the future and this explains the love for children which so many of them share. A great and profound love for children runs like a thread through the whole of Gorky's life.

This is borne out by Gorky's splendid letters to children. To paraphrase them is impossible. The only course is to quote two of them.

One letter was written long ago, before the revolution, and that is why it speaks about the letter *Yat*.* It was written in Capri and addressed to "The School of Jolly Children"—a kindergarten in Baku.

Here is the letter:

"When I read your letter I laughed so heartily that all the fishes poked their noses out of the water to find out whatever could have put me in such a jolly mood. I explained to them what splendid people there were living on the shores of another sea, that they were still quite small but that I felt certain that when they grew

---

* *Yat* — the thirtieth letter in the old Russian alphabet. It was very often confounded by school children with the vowel "e" both of which were pronounced alike. It was deleted after the revolution, when the new alphabet was adopted.—*Trans.*

up they would be just as fine, and that was why I was so happy.

"So that you shouldn't be able to say my handwriting is so bad you can't make head or tail of it, I wrote this letter on a typewriter.

"But how do you write yourselves? You just wait! I'm going to put these letters of yours away and in, say, twenty years from now I'll show them to you and then you'll see what amazing things you used to write once.

"I'd like to know, for instance, what is: turtell? laisy? duzzen? speltakle?

"Even I don't play such tricks with the Russian language as you do!

"My weak point is when to use the letter *yat*—only please don't give me away to anybody!

"This letter always worries me and whenever I have to use it I feel as though I am not forty but only four years of age.

"Even in such words as *pyat, podnyat, ponyat* I am always haunted by this *yat*, so that instead of *pyat* I write *pet*! *

"How I should like to see you, my dear children. What fun it would be to romp and play together, and what wonderful and funny stories I could tell you! Although I'm not so young now I assure you I'm not such a dull fellow and I'm not at all bad at showing what happens to a samovar when you put hot coals into the funnel and forget to pour in the water. I could also show you how a lazy and stupid fish takes the bait, and plenty of other funny tricks. I love to play with children. It's an old habit of mine. When I was about ten years old I had to look after my younger brother—he has died since. Later on I had to look after two other tiny tots,

---

* *Pyat*—five; *podnyat* — raise; *ponyat* — understand; *pet*— sing.—*Trans.*

and after that, when I was about twenty, I used to round up all the children who lived in my street and go off with them on a Sunday for the whole day, from early in the morning until late in the evening.

"It was really splendid, you know! There'd be a crowd of about sixty children, all quite young—between about four and ten. And they'd romp about in the woods until more often than not they would be too tired to walk home.

"But I was always prepared for such an emergency. I had a chair with shoulder straps. And I would strap the chair to my back and give a lift to the children who were too tired to walk and so take them home across the fields. Oh, it was wonderful!

"Yes, it was a jolly time and I always recall it with pleasure. And after that I became a writer, which is a very difficult job indeed, although I'm very fond of it."

The second letter, which was written in our times, was addressed to the pupils of a school in Irkutsk that had been named after him:

"Comrade Basov came to see me and told me all about the splendid schools that are being built in Eastern Siberia, also about the progress you were making and what a lot of talent there was amongst you.

"I was especially glad to hear that you were working hard, painstakingly. That is how it should be, children. One must love science, for men have no mightier and no more victorious weapon than science. The working people of our world have paid with untold suffering for their ignorance and illiteracy. Your fathers have flung open to you the broad road that leads to the pinnacles of science and on you now devolves the duty of carrying on what your fathers began. Eighteen years of courageous efforts, of heroic striving, is a living testimony of the miracles which the proletariat, the masters of the country, can perform with the help of science....

"We need hundreds of thousands of doctors, teachers, engineers, musicians, actors, poets, writers and so on and so forth, an army of people who will devote their energy to exploring and developing the treasures hidden in the bowels of the earth. In our country there can be no place for parasites which endanger people's health, or weeds which sap the vitality of the earth, or pests which do damage to forests and grain. We must cultivate the whole of our land like a garden, drain swamps, water the deserts, dig canals, dredge river beds, build millions of miles of roads and clear our vast forests. There must be no place in our country for locusts which destroy our grain, for mosquitoes which infect people with fevers, for flies which are the bearers of various diseases, for pests which are a veritable plague to our livestock. Rats and mice—these parasites cause us losses which run into hundreds of millions of rubles, as also do the rodents of the fields—moles, marmots and field mice. This, of course, is not all. There are plenty of other fields of endeavour, joyous work in building up and developing the first truly cultured, Socialist state. This is the work that awaits you and it demands the broadest possible scientific knowledge."

It was on behalf of this joyous work, which was to transform the future into the present, dreams into reality, that the great proletarian writer lived, wrote and fought.

And it is with these lines, which are addressed to those to whom the future of our country belongs, that I would like to close this short biography of Maxim Gorky.

www.ingramcontent.com/pod-product-compliance
Lightning Source LLC
Chambersburg PA
CBHW011951150426
43195CB00018B/2891